Gourmet Cooking with Homemade Wines

Gourmet Cooking with Homemade Wines

Warner & Lucile Bowers

Stackpole Books

GOURMET COOKING WITH HOMEMADE WINES

Copyright © 1975 by
Warner and Lucile Bowers

Published by
STACKPOLE BOOKS
Cameron and Kelker Streets
Harrisburg, Pa. 17105

Printed in the U.S.A.

Library of Congress Cataloging in Publication Data

Bowers, Warner Fremont, 1906-
    Gourmet cooking with homemade wines.

    Includes index.
    1. Cookery (Wine)   2. Wine and wine making.
I. Bowers, Lucile, 1905-   II. Title.
TX726.B63   641.6'2   75-9818
ISBN 0-8117-0739-3

Contents

Chapter 7   Lamb   107

roast leg of lamb / lamb shank stews from around the
world / lamb patties / cassoulet / lamb steaks / lamb
ragout

Chapter 8   Poultry   117

cornish game hens / roulades of chicken breast / wine-
injected turkey breast / braised chicken halves / cinnamon chicken halves / chicken mole poblano /
chicken paprikash / chicken ground nut stew / Chinese
almond chicken / coq au vin / turkey chow mein /
turkey pot pie / roast turkey with corn bread stuffing /
roast Long Island duckling with raspberry wine sauce /
chicken pan American / chicken with green sauce /
stuffings for fowl

Chapter 9   Seafood   137

roulades of sole / baked whole red snapper / shrimp tarragon / shrimp Stroganoff / braised shad roe / vatapa
fish stew / cioppino / coquilles St. Jacques / shrimp en
coquille / poached and broiled shad roe / fresh cod and
salmon croquettes / fish quiche

Chapter 10   Specialty Meats   149

sauerkraut and knockwurst / sherried chicken livers on
English muffins / sweetbreads Mornay in patty shells /
braised sweetbreads / beef and kidney pie / regal liver
and onions / liver parmigiana / braised hare / stuffed
beef heart / spiced tongue / calves' brains

Chapter 11   Treats from the Barbecue Grill   159

barbecued Long Island duckling / hickory-broiled steak
with wine marinade / double-thick pork chops with
wine sauce / grilled chicken quarters / grilled lobster
tails with wine sauce / grilled steak teriyaki / royal
hamburgers / london broil with curry-wine steak sauce
/ breast of chicken en brochette / lamb shashlik /
scallops en brochette / beef-kidney shish kebab /
shrimp en brochette / lobster-steak combo

PART II
MAKING YOUR OWN COOKING AND TABLE WINES

Acknowledgments

Some of the material published in this book has appeared in *The Purple Thumb Magazine* and in *Home Beer and Winemaking Magazine*. We are grateful to the editors of these magazines for permission to use that material in modified and expanded form. The photograph appearing on the front of the jacket of this book is by Joseph Zottarelli.

Part 1

RECIPES FOR
ELEGANT EATING

~~~~~~

CHAPTER 1

Basic Techniques in Gourmet Cooking

Of course, "gourmet" is not listed in any dictionary as an adjective. The noun comes from an ancient French word referring to a winemaker's boy apprentice. So, "gourmet cooking" can mean almost anything you want it to mean. To most people, gourmet cooking means something outrageously expensive, highly exotic, terribly complicated to prepare, or all three. We use the term to mean excellent food, well but simply prepared, with emphasis on subtle twists in seasoning, addition of various kinds of wine, and unusual combinations of ingredients. Our interest arose gradually and somewhat serendipitously.

First, the organic garden provided more fruits, vegetables, and herbs than we could use, store, or give away. One obvious answer was, "Make wine!" But after we realized we were filling the shelves with gallon jugs of twenty-eight kinds of wine, it was apparent that even sitting around drinking wine all day would put only a small dent in the stock. Again, the obvious answer was

"Cook with it!" Well-known as iconoclasts, we began to devise our own recipes or to modify others to include generous amounts of wine. The result was so astounding that magazine articles naturally followed, two editors asked for a steady regular series of these stories, and this stimulated more diversification until our recipes ran the gamut from hors d'oeuvres through soups and salads to entrees and desserts.

Always interested in the hows and whys as well as the search for simple methods, we gradually accumulated many knacks and tricks which do things better and more easily. With no pretense of either completeness or profundity, we share what we know of many basic procedures.

Marinades and How to Use Them

The process of marinating foods, principally chunks of meat, began in the prerefrigeration era, when a carcass was hung in the coolest, breeziest spot available in order to slow the inevitable deterioration. Thus originated the saying, "The goose hangs high," to indicate that at the moment, all is well. As the aroma began to change from pleasant to offensive, there was a period when some attempt at disguise of odor and flavor was needed. Soaking meats in wine was the best answer, particularly when strong and pungent spices were added.

In more primitive times, wild game made up the meat supply and marinating was needed to mellow the gamy taste. And when animals were domesticated, it usually was the older, nonmilk-producing, inefficient draft animal which ended up on the dinner table. Here, not only was the strong flavor disguised but tough, stringy meat became somewhat edible. Wine, and especially its alcohol content, acts directly on protein, causing it to swell and thus become more tender. The dense white fibrous tissue is softened also. Thus, marinades not only cover up unpleasant flavors and odors but they add new flavors of their own at the same time that they tenderize tough cuts of meat.

Marinating really is a form of preliminary cooking because the marinade gradually coagulates the protein by acid or alcohol action, whereas cooking does the same thing more rapidly and thoroughly by heat. In warmer climes where more food is eaten cold, it was discovered that the acid of lime juice will solidly coagulate protein such as fish or other seafood. This became the ceviche of many countries as well as the lomilomi salmon of the South Pacific islands. The acid is used up by oxidation during the marinating process so that nonacid compounds are formed and the end result tastes tart but not sour. The typical marinade is acidic, usually based on vinegar or the alcohol in wine. An example of vinegar marinade is the sauerbraten of the Germans or some of the rabbit dishes.

Originally, most meats were roasted over an open fire; so there was no opportunity to cook the marinade with the meat. But primitive peoples as well as most modern Europeans knew that blood is pure protein and not to be wasted. As cooking containers developed, the marinade with its contained blood was used in baking the meat. The original marinade or the resulting cooking juices was used in soups, stews, sauces, and gravies. Today, usually only the vinegar marinades are discarded although they too can be used with discretion, the sour taste being lost largely by reaction with the meat or by the heat of cooking.

The purpose of marinating with wine today is not to disguise the natural flavor of the meat or tenderize it but to add to its flavor as well as increase its succulence. It is usual to cover the meat about halfway with the marinade, spoon it over the meat at intervals, or turn the piece of meat periodically. Marinating at room temperature, even overnight, is safe in a covered container because the alcohol or vinegar prevents spoilage. For longer periods, marinating, covered, in the refrigerator is best. The better the cut of meat, the shorter the period of marinating needed; and with prime meat, pouring wine over it at cooking time gives the desired result without the need for long soaking.

Ordinarily, red meat takes a robust red wine as marinade and in most cases, white meats take a white or rosé wine, but this is not absolute since Coq au Vin (see chapter 8) calls for red wine. Also, we use all sorts of flavor combinations such as quince wine with lamb, plum or tea with beef, peach or pear with pork, angelica with chicken, and so on. There are no hard and fast rules as to which wine to use or for how long. But, be sure to

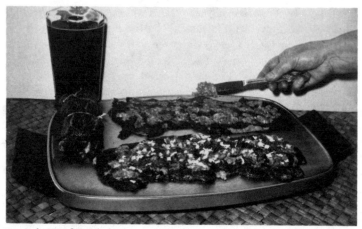

To make Beef Roulades (see chapter 4), take a generous but thin slice of top round and spread it with a layer of hot sausage followed by a good sprinkle of chopped onion. The rolled and securely tied roulade is braised in one of the red wines (shown here is cabernet).

use the marinade in preparing the finished dish, either as a sauce or gravy.

Finally, marinating of fruit is purely to enhance flavor although eye-appeal sometimes is improved. We cut up various fruits of the season or as many kinds as the garden affords and marinate the compote in several ways. Sherry, brandy, rum, champagne, or a bland white wine are all excellent; but we prefer a marinade of liqueur such as almond, cherry, peach, lemon, rose, or orange. Cover the fruit pieces about halfway, turn the pieces, and marinate for an hour or so before refrigerating. Serve in hollow-stem champagne glasses and do not be shy about drinking the liquid. Even the best people do it.

How to Stuff Chops, Roasts, and Flank Steaks

The stuffing of cuts of meat probably is an offshoot of larding, whereby dry roasts were made more succulent by lacing them internally with strips of fat pulled through by a larding needle or crammed into stab wounds made with a long, thin-bladed knife. Naturally, from this process it was an easy and logical step to progress to stuffing in one's favorite ingredients. Internal larding is much more efficient and satisfactory than barding, which consists of covering a roast with sheets of fat or strips of blanched bacon.

For stuffing, chops should be at least 1½ inches thick. The secret of success is in preparing the pocket properly. If done incorrectly, the chop will open during cooking and spill its stuffing. With a long, thin boning knife, make a small cut no longer than a teaspoon width, at the tip (narrow end) of the chop, close to the bone. Gradually work the knife around inside the chop so that the largest possible pocket is made without cutting through to the outside at any point and without enlarging the opening slit. It is difficult to skewer-close such thick chops after stuffing, and sewing them shut is too much trouble, but with the small opening properly placed, closure is not needed anyway.

In roasts, multiple small stab-wounds are better than trying to make one large pocket. Whether the stabs are made horizontally or perpendicularly is not terribly important except that the horizontal incisions tend to leak more fluid during cooking than do the vertical ones. Small cuts usually are made but any size is acceptable as long as it will accommodate what is to be stuffed

To make the pocket for stuffing a double-thick pork chop, insert the knife next to the bone at the rib end and carefully enlarge the internal cut. The dish of stuffing is the same as that used for the large fluted mushroom caps.

into it. A little-used variety of "stuffing" is to wrap a very choice piece of meat inside a cut of lesser grade and sew it in place. This method was formerly used in the original Château Briand, where a beef tenderloin was sewed inside something like a piece of flank steak. No one bothers with this nowadays.

The usual flank steak is too thin to permit the making of a slit-pocket but there are two alternatives. First, the entire flank steak may be spread or covered with whatever stuffing is preferred. Then the whole thing is tightly rolled and tied many times around with string to make a giant roulade, served in slices. The other method is to fold the flank steak in the middle and sew all edges, leaving only a small opening through which the very large cavity can be stuffed. By this method, so much stuffing can be inserted that the whole thing becomes football-shaped and almost football-sized. This is very interesting and unusual when baked and served in slices.

These various pockets lend themselves to insertion of all sorts of dressings, forcemeats, and stuffings; or, if preferred, whole baby carrots, small white onions, tiny potatoes, other vegetables, or even whole hard-boiled eggs can be inserted.

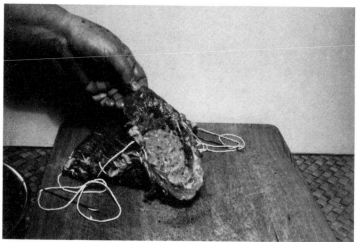

Leaving the side sewing strings long on the flank steak makes it easier to close the pocket completely after the stuffing has been inserted.

How to Inject Roasts with Wine

We frequently use a cross between marinating and stuffing in what might be called internal marinade. We have always had a poor opinion of the very dry white meat of poultry breast and were moved to do something about it. Since the skin largely nullifies attempts at marinating in wine, we hit upon the idea of using a large syringe and needle to inject wine throughout the flesh before baking. This is not as easy as it sounds because the flesh is very dense and requires a lot of pressure for very little injection. It is a somewhat hazardous procedure also, because the pressure is forever blowing the syringe off the needle with resulting deluge of the environs by wine. We usually compromise by injecting most of the wine under the skin, thus keeping the meat very moist and toothsome. We manage to get a cup of wine into a 10-pound piece of turkey breast, and we rarely if ever cook a whole turkey anymore.

Roasts other than turkey breast can be injected but it is not easy, and without any covering skin, the wine tends to leak out during cooking. Turkey breast injection really is our best effort in this line. However, if you do roast whole turkeys, be sure to

Plum wine is injected into a turkey breast with the needle which screws onto the end of a baster. About a cup of wine can be injected, especially under the skin, where the tissues are looser.

inject the thighs and legs liberally. Of course, this takes more than just the one cupful.

The Knack of Mixing Hot Liquids with Eggs

This may be very elementary to many housewives but, properly done, it means the difference between a smooth sauce and some form of wet scrambled eggs or a soup. To make a smooth sauce, it is essential to heat the eggs gradually, this being done by adding a little of the hot liquid at a time to the beaten eggs, continuing to beat all the while. Eventually, when all the hot liquid has been added, a very smooth result will have been attained without curdling or lumping.

The reverse procedure, adding beaten eggs to hot liquid while beating, gives a lumpy result; but adding the eggs while only stirring has a definite place. This is the way to form the "egg flowers" used with such pleasing effect in the eggdrop soup of the Chinese or the avgolemono (lemon soup) of the Greeks.

Baking Tart and Pie Shells

Many types of pies and tarts call for a prebaked shell and still others, in order to avoid soaking of the crust, require a partially baked shell before the filling is added and the baking is finished. An annoying habit of these tart and pie shells is to buckle in the center or in other ways become misshapen. Sugar often causes these complications. When two tablespoons of sugar are added to regular piecrust dough, tart dough results which, when made into a shell for prebaking, not only persists in popping up in the middle but has walls which tend to sag and melt down before baking sets them.

All of these problems can be avoided by one of the following two methods. First, after the dough is shaped in the pan, set another, empty pie tin inside the first on top of the dough to hold it in place. Now bake. Or shape the dough in a pie tin, mold on a sheet of aluminum foil to fit, and then fill this with dry rice or beans and bake. The rice or beans will hold the shell in place, will not change the taste, are reusable, and can later be cooked as usual.

Blanching and Stir-Frying Vegetables

The contrast between American and Chinese methods of preparing vegetables is startling. The cook-it-to-death-with-a-hamhock method, often practiced in the South, doubtless has virtues for tough green leaves. However, just as many meats are tender and juicy when served rare but tough and dry as sole leather when overcooked, so many vegetables need only the briefest exposure to heat in order to remain delightfully crisp and yet lose that green, slightly bitter taste. The Chinese are past masters in the art of quick-cooking vegetables, but possibly this is more a matter of necessity than anything else. Cooking over a charcoal brazier requires mostly quick-cooking dishes, while an old wood-burning range will permit the boiling of turnip leaves and other defenseless vegetables for days on end.

We are thoroughly addicted to the Chinese system of blanching and stir-frying whereby most green vegetables are thrown into a very hot iron pan (wok) with a little cooking oil and tossed for a few moments until the vegetables are heated through, oil-coated, and slightly changed in color. Few if any vitamins are lost by this method.

Making and preserving Bouillon

A tremendous amount of very valuable protein is thrown away by most Americans but not by us! The lost protein is gelatin from the skin, meat scraps, and bones of chicken, duck, turkey, and goose. We always save all carcass elements: bones, skin, scraps of meat, necks, and cooking juices. We barely cover these with water and boil slowly until everything except the bones falls to pieces. Then we strain, cool, refrigerate, and scoop off the layer of hardened fat. The chicken fat goes into a freezer container to accumulate until we make chicken liver pâté. The other fat accumulates in cans in the refrigerator to be added to crumbs and seeds as bird banquets for winter months.

From two cornish game hens or a turkey breast carcass, we get about a quart of strained bouillon which is so rich in protein that it gels firmly and can be used as an aspic. This bouillon can be kept in the refrigerator, preferably with a thin film of hardened fat on the surface. If it is not used up in a week, we boil the bouillon vigorously for a few minutes and then it is good for another week of refrigeration.

Sometimes we get a little too much bouillon on hand and then we freeze it, in which state it keeps indefinitely. We freeze the bouillon in small quantities so it is not necessary to thaw a large container just to get a small amount. One very convenient method is to freeze bouillon in ice cube trays and knock out the bouillon cubes for storage in plastic bags. A little experimentation will show how many bouillon ice cubes it takes to make a cupful or some other convenient measurement.

We are firm believers in the virtues of water for bathing and for laundry, but we think its wide use in cooking is a little unimaginative. We usually boil vegetables in bouillon, always use the latter instead of water in stews, and alternate between wine and bouillon or use a combination of them in cooking. In a few instances when chicken flavor is not desirable, we just add beef bouillon cubes or beef extract to the chicken bouillon. Much less useful is court bouillon, which we make from fish bones, scraps, and skin. We have relatively few uses for court bouillon, but we use chicken bouillon by the gallon. One very important use for bouillon is in covering chicken, turkey, or duck before freezing. This prevents the meat from drying out and losing its flavor.

Charcoal and Hickory-Smoke Barbecue

Although many people speak ecstatically of hickory-smoke barbecue, their experience is largely in catering to voracious kids of all ages, gorging on hot dogs and hamburgers. Furthermore, they do not know what hickory smoke is all about. Charcoal briquettes usually are made from oakwood but no matter; charcoal burns with a red-white heat and there is no smoke except from the charring meat and the burning fat drippings. What most people speak of as hickory flavor is just burned meat and the aroma of burned fat. This is very good but it is not hickory.

We sliver short lengths of pencil-sized wood from a hickory log and soak the slivers in water so they will smoke and smolder without flaming. When the charcoal fire has burned to a bed of coals, we place four or more of these wet slivers on the surface and then put the meat on the grill. The fragrant smoke is delightful and the rare meat is delicately flavored by the time it is ready. With an adjustable grill, the meat can be smoked on the raised grill before lowering it to cooking height.

We had an interesting experience with this process while stopping at Kula Lodge on the side of the volcano Haleakala on the Hawaiian island of Maui. At 4:30 P.M. the manager asked how we wanted our dinner steak and our choice was rare, for dinner at seven. He immediately started the fire in an outdoor grill and, much to our consternation, covered the charcoal with wattle chips from an Australian tree. In a few moments, he hung the steaks in the smoke and we had visions of very well-done steak in another couple of hours. To his everlasting credit, the steaks were very rare and deliciously flavored at seven!

How to Make Coconut Milk and Cream

Years of tropical and subtropical living have given us a strong taste for the flavor of coconut. We have been pleased that so many recipes from Africa, South America, the Pacific islands, and the Asiatic countries call for coconut milk. This is not the water from inside a coconut, as so many suppose.

To make coconut milk, crack a nut and remove the meat, which will come out easily if the shell is put in a warm oven for about fifteen minutes. Shave off the brown layer with a vegetable peeler, break the meat into small pieces, and put all the meat into a blender with two cups of boiling water. Blend at high speed until fairly smooth. The time-honored method then calls for straining out the pulp, but we prefer to leave it in the milk.

Coconut milk can be kept frozen indefinitely and we only make a quantity about twice a year. We freeze the coconut milk in small amounts because most recipes call for not over half a cup. If you strain out the pulp, do not discard it but serve it over ice cream with shavings of chocolate.

Coconut cream is made in the same way except that you use half as much water, getting a much thicker and fattier result, high in calories.

Cornstarch Versus Flour Thickening

Methods of thickening soups, gravies, and sauces conform to availability of different starches in various countries. In the Asiatic countries, rice flour naturally was favored while in Europe, potato or manioc flour was more prevalent. In America, the choices have been largely between cornstarch and wheat flour. In most recent years, the choices almost everywhere have shifted to cornstarch and wheat flour, largely because of ready availability.

Wheat flour as a thickening agent formerly had to be used as a paste in milk or water because of its tendency to form lumps, the bane of serious chefs. The modern all-purpose no-sift flour can be shaken dry into a liquid with very little fear of lumping but it must be cooked for a short period to do away with the "raw" taste and the resulting sauce is opaque, which offends chefs.

Cornstarch, on the other hand, is the usual choice of chefs even though its lumping tendencies are worse than those of wheat flour ever were. But cornstarch, added as a thin paste in water or milk, need be cooked only until the sauce thickens. Besides, it becomes clear and is tasteless. The clarity appeals to chefs.

We use either wheat flour or cornstarch: wheat flour for ordinary purposes and cornstarch when a clear sauce seems important. Sometimes we make the starch paste in bouillon and sometimes we use wine as the liquid. A time-honored way to thicken sauces is by first making a roux, which is flour and butter fried together until the flour is done but still white. Additional cooking forms the brown roux which is used to thicken dark sauces. Sometimes mirepoix is added to the roux or later to the sauce for its flavor and also for thickening. Mirepoix is made by sautéing finely chopped onion, celery, and carrot together until soft but not brown. It is the basis for the wonderful sauce of Osso Buco (see chapter 6) and some other stews.

An elegant thickener is duxelles, made by sautéing finely chopped mushrooms in butter until a very firm state, almost a paste, is attained. This is flavored with nutmeg, mace, and allspice. Added to sauces and some forcemeats, it is a delicious contribution.

Varied Uses of Ground Meats

There are many similarities and overlapping terms in this category. Ground meats with a high proportion of fat and a lot of herb seasonings are sausage; run through the grinder another time, they become forcemeats, if fed into casings; if ground a third time and baked in a *bain marie* (water bath), they are pâtés; with alternating strips of meat and forcemeat, baked in a bath, they are terrines, but ground only once and simply baked in a pan, they are the lowly meatloaf. Some slight change in preparation or cooking procedure makes all the difference. A similar mixture with a high proportion of bread cubes or crumbs, cracker crumbs, cornmeal, or crumbled corn bread, with addition of various fruits, nuts, and herbs, becomes dressing or stuffing, if you prefer that term.

Ground meat for sausage, pâté, terrine, meatloaf, or meat balls usually is some combination of beef, pork, and veal with the very occasional addition of fowl or some specialty meat such as tongue or liver. The magic is wrought by subtle changes in wines and seasonings. The addition of wine varies in volume, depending on whether there are crumbs to absorb the liquid. A pure meat mixture will not take up much wine but the juices come out in cooking, leaving the flavor; so no harm is done. The standby seasoning is sage, but the Swedish use aromatic spices such as nutmeg and mace with the more occasional allspice, while the Italians use oregano, thyme, and even parmesan cheese. Dishes containing liver profit greatly from the addition of allspice and black pepper. Specific recipes will be given at appropriate places in the later chapters.

Freezing and Thawing Foods

Misinformation and misconceptions about the freezing and thawing of foods are widespread. Whenever our freezer breaks down, the repairman gloatingly offers to remove all of our frozen foods with the prospect that we may recover some small fraction of its value in insurance while he sits at home and eats our wonderful food. We simply get some frozen carbon dioxide (dry ice) and ride it out till repairs are made. Foods do not necessarily spoil if they thaw, but there are a few points to remember. Thawed foods will keep under refrigeration just as long as if they had not been frozen. Simple thawing does not cause spoilage, which depends on the presence of growing bacteria or molds or both. Meats can be refrozen just as well as not, if they have been kept refrigerated after thawing and if not kept longer than any other food in the refrigerator. Some foods should not be refrozen, simply because they have physically changed on thawing. For example, berries tend to become mushy and do not reconstitute on refreezing. Leafy and soft items tend to lose shape and identity, looking unsightly but not necessarily spoiling. They could be creamed or made into soufflé. Disposing of foods that have thawed temporarily is just as senseless as the old belief that material had to be removed immediately from an opened can, else "ptomaine poisoning" would surely do you in. Tin cans of themselves are not poisonous nor is thawed food which is kept cold.

Small-Quantity Freezing

We freeze in small quantities, not that we fear the effects of thawing and refreezing, but simply for speed and convenience. For example, we freeze Chinese snow peas with the edible pods in plastic sandwich bags with just enough for a Chinese dish for two persons in each bag. All the bags of peas then are put into one large plastic bag so we can tell when we are reaching the end of the supply.

We grow rather luxuriant crops of berries and these we spread dry on cooky sheets to freeze. The individual dry frozen berries then are stored in two-quart freezer containers. Berries for thawing and use can be removed individually, by the cupful, or in any quantity needed without having to thaw a whole container.

Freezing bouillon in ice cube trays has been mentioned and is another example of small-quantity freezing to make availability quicker and more simple. Similarly, we freeze special leftover chunks of cooked lamb, pork, and turkey, usually freezing them in their own cooking juices and saving them until enough variety has accumulated to make a casserole of the French baked bean dish, Cassoulet (see chapter 7).

Also, we buy various cuts of meat which we trim into better shape, using the trimmed portions for medallions, tips, cutlets, chafing dish steak, or for grinding. These special cuts are frozen in plastic bags, by type, in amounts required for a meal for two persons.

Perpetual Soup Pot for Leftovers

We know of a lady who baby-sits for neighbors and is in great demand because she always cleans out the refrigerator to make a marvelous pot of soup which she leaves for the family. We have improved on this plan by not letting leftovers accumulate haphazardly in the refrigerator in the first place. We actually have two parts to our plan.

In our freezer there always are several two-quart plastic containers labelled "for soup." Into these go leftover meats, gravies and sauces, vegetables, and even pasta. To make a great soup in what we call our perpetual pot, we just empty two of the two-quart blocks of frozen leftovers, cover with bouillon, add barley or dried peas, and bring to a slow boil. Even though no two batches of soup are identical, we vary the flavor still further by appropriate seasoning. One batch may be flavored with Angostura bitters and cayenne, another with homemade curry powder, a third with Italian spices, still another with cumin and chili powder, while a fifth may be seasoned with allspice, cloves, and nutmeg. The perpetual soup pot can be kept in the refrigerator and, since the soup is brought to a boil at least once a week, it keeps without problems. A particularly long-lasting soup may be frozen. This solves the leftover problem and gives us a never ending variety of delicious hearty soups.

Preserving Spices and Condiments

Dry preserving is extremely simple in some climates, requires special equipment in some areas, and may be entirely unsuitable in very humid regions. Methods vary from simple air exposure to complicated controlled ovens. We use drying mainly for herbs, of which we grow at least eighteen varieties for our own use. Hanging the plants upside down in an attic for weeks is perfectly acceptable as a means of drying but requires an attic! We prefer the oven of the kitchen stove, set at "warm," with the herbs spread thinly on cooky sheets. The required drying time varies widely from twenty minutes to an hour, depending on the type of herb; the process is complete when the leaves are crumbly. As soon as the leaves cool, we crumble them, put them in small spice bottles, close tightly, and store in a dark place. Our herbs keep their flavor for at least four years by this method.

Many herbs lose their strength when dried but simple freezing is not satisfactory because the soft green leaves thaw to an unsightly mush. For a favorite herb such as French tarragon or for coriander, a rapid strength-loser, we whirl the herb in the blender and then freeze the puree. Ordinarily, just enough water is added to make a very heavy puree, or mayonnaise may be substituted. Puree in salad oil also is suitable, the choice depending upon how the puree is to be used. Frozen purees seem to keep indefinitely.

Some herbs do not freeze well, lose their zest when dried, and are not always available fresh. Coriander (also known as cilantro or Chinese parsley) is one of these but we found one answer in an alcohol extract, made like all the flavor extracts sold in stores. We fill a small spice jar with herb leaves, fill with vodka, close tightly, and set the bottle away for a few weeks. Usually, this extract is strong enough so that the same leaves can be extracted again by refilling the bottle with vodka. This method is useful also for herbs which remain unpleasantly firm to bite, such as bay leaves or those which look unsightly in a white-type sauce. Similarly, vodka extracts of flowers, such as American Beauty roses, can be preserved for use in baking or in making cordials.

It is remarkable how long simple vinegar-salt or vinegar-sugar mixtures will preserve fruits and vegetables in a closed container in the refrigerator. Using this method, we have kept mango, peach, and pear chutneys in 2-quart plastic containers in the refrigerator for periodic use over 4 years without spoilage. Eventually, caponata, with its somewhat lower vinegar content, tended to mold, but only after two years of refrigeration. We keep many fresh vegetables for salad all winter long in glass 2-quart jars filled with 4 parts vinegar to 1 part water, with 1 tablespoon of salt per pint. Vegetables such as kohlrabi, girasols, carrots, celery, cauliflower, raw potatoes, tiny green tomatoes, and mushrooms do well in this manner, even on the kitchen shelf with no refrigeration.

Homemade wines and liqueurs can be a form of herb-preserving also, closely related to the alcohol extract method but more widely applicable to cooking in many ways. We have used angelica, woodruff, and lemon balm in wine thus far and have used rose, anise, angelica, lemon balm, and tarragon in liqueurs for baking and desserts.

Warming Plates and Serving Dishes

Foods meant to be eaten hot should be served quite hot and should remain at least warm throughout the meal. There are few things more unappetizing than to watch the fat slowly congeal on the plate right under your very eyes. Lamb is particularly troublesome in this regard since the fat very rapidly hardens.

Most people think to use roll-warming devices at table but the usual cookbook phrase, "Transfer to a preheated platter," leaves them cold, if you can pardon the pun. Still more unusual is the preheating of dinner plates, which is routine with us except when eating from individual ramekins or soup pots. Time of year no longer has any real bearing on the problem because with air conditioning, our dining room actually is cooler in summer than in winter. Therefore, we heat plates and serving platters all year around.

There are fancy electric trays and insulated bags designed for heating plates, but we have not found them necessary. Our warming tray is used entirely to keep certain hors d'oeuvres hot at cocktail time. Hot rolls remain edible simply by being covered with a folded cloth napkin. Most electric dishwashers can be started or stopped at any point in their cycle and so, by starting in the dish-drying part of the cycle, you can use the circulating hot air as an efficient plate and platter warmer. We do not use this method but it is simple to do. Of course, some stoves have a plate-warming compartment. Too, it is possible to use the regular oven, but since we have only one oven, ours is usually full of cooking food, without room for stacks of dishes.

The simplest way we have found is to stack dishes and platters in the sink and slowly run the hottest water over them. We arrange the dishes so that the water cascades from top to bottom and all plates get piping hot. Dried and stacked just at serving time, they keep food at just the right temperature.

~~~~~~

CHAPTER 2

Hors d'Oeuvres, Brunch, and Cocktail Buffet

Like many Americans, we are as addicted to predinner pâtés and spreads as we are to our daily limit of one cocktail, usually a martini. Even in the throes of a periodic weight-reducing program, we usually find some good excuse for not changing the predinner routine too drastically. By alternating ten or more homemade wines in four or five kinds of cheese or with shrimp and chicken livers, we get an almost endless variety of culinary surprises which double in delightful and interesting gourmet ways.

SHRIMP PÂTÉ   *Vermouth or White Grape Wine*

Our shrimp pâté is adapted from an old southern recipe for Sunday brunch, but we find it excellent on crackers as an hors d'oeuvre. It makes a very tasty tiny cocktail sandwich and it really shines as a filling for a fancy brunch omelette. Here is how we make it.

> About 1 lb cooked shrimp, put through fine blade of food grinder while still frozen hard
> 8 tbsp melted butter
> 2 tbsp vermouth or catawba grape wine
> 4 tbsp fresh lemon juice
> 4 tbsp dry instant minced onion
> ½ tsp ground mace
> ½ tsp dry mustard
> ½ tsp powdered cayenne
> 2 tsp salt
> ½ tsp ground white pepper

We find that the shrimp grind finer when frozen; after grinding, we let them thaw, pouring off any excess liquid and letting them come to room temperature. Use white pepper so that it will not look as though you forgot to devein the shrimp.

Add the melted butter to all the other ingredients, mixing

The serendipitous pâtés—cheese, chicken liver, and shrimp—are served as spreads on crackers with cocktails, but they double as elegant omelette fillings on other occasions.

thoroughly to a smooth consistency. The onions are added dry so that they will take moisture, but excess juice still may have to be removed with a spoon, later. Let the pâté stand for several hours in the refrigerator to blend the spices and then package for the freezer except for one crock for current use. This pâté will keep for at least six months frozen.

CHICKEN LIVER PÂTÉ *Chianti*

We modified this recipe from one which called for Canadian goose liver. After all, who has Canadian goose livers except, possibly, Canadian geese?

> About 2 lb chicken livers, cooked 20 minutes and drained
> 1 cup shortening (using ½ cup butter and ½ cup chicken fat, if possible)
> ½ cup dry instant minced onion
> 1½ tsp dry mustard
> 2 tsp salt
> ¼ tsp ground cloves
> ¼ tsp nutmeg
> ¼ tsp ground allspice
> ½ tsp ground black pepper
> 2 tbsp chianti or red grape wine
> 1 6-oz can mushroom stems and pieces, chopped fine

Sieve the chicken livers while hot into the melted butter and chicken fat. Add all the other ingredients and mix thoroughly. Let stand in the refrigerator several hours for the spices to blend. Then package in crocks and freeze all but one crock. The onions are used dry in order to absorb moisture and make the pâté firmer. If too firm, work in a little more wine. Remember that refrigeration will solidify the butter; so get the pâté out half an hour before use.

FISH SPREAD and PÂTÉ *Chenin Blanc*

Fish spread, with us, usually is a serendipitous treat when we broil more fish than we can eat at one meal. Almost always, we use swordfish or one of the flat fish such as sole or flounder. The fatty fishes we do not use because of their much stronger taste. Fish spread can be a very simple but excellent dish, since the meat is already cooked.

To make fish spread, finely flake any available quantity of cooked dry fish meat. Moisten with white wine and work into a smooth paste. Add tartar sauce and continue to work until the mixture will adhere and hold its shape. Pack into a fancy-shaped mold and refrigerate. To serve, unmold onto a platter surrounded by cocktail crackers. A dash of nutmeg, mace, or paprika over the top makes a nice festive appearance.

A good fish pâté, made from raw fish and baked, is made as follows:

> 2 lb raw white fish meat, blended to a paste
> 4 egg whites
> 2 tbsp cornstarch
> 2 tbsp white wine
> 24 water chestnuts, chopped
> ¼ tsp coriander extract
> 2 tsp soy sauce
> 1 tsp fresh ginger, chopped
> ½ cup green onions and tops, chopped

Mix all the ingredients thoroughly and pack into a loaf pan, or several tiny pans for a more elegant appearance. Bake in a water bath in a 350-degree oven for 2 hours or until a toothpick comes out clean. Let cool, unmold, and refrigerate if the pâté is to be served cold, sliced.

PÂTÉ MAISON BOWERS   *Zinfandel*

The only thing that prevents this from being a simple meat loaf is that we run it through the fine blade of the meat grinder three times, add wine, and floss it up with spices. It is excellent hot or cold, with cocktails, as a pre-entree course, or in sandwiches. By any name, it is very good.

Triply grind meat in the proportion of ½ beef, ¼ pork, and ¼ veal to a total of about 2 pounds. Put the ground meat in a large bowl and add the following ingredients:

1 tsp salt per pound of meat
2 tbsp hot sauce (A-1, worcestershire, Pick-A-Pepper,
   Picante, etc.)
1 tbsp Angostura bitters
1 cup onion, finely chopped
½ cup red wine or substitute brandy
½ tsp each black pepper, cayenne, nutmeg, dry mustard,
   cinnamon, cloves, allspice, bay leaf, coriander
12 drops lemon oil or peel of 1 lemon, finely chopped

Mix very thoroughly until quite homogeneous. Pack into a loaf pan, set this in a water bath, and bake in a 350-degree oven for about 2 hours or until the juices are clear.

CHICKEN PÂTÉ   *Sherry Amoroso*

The fancier pâtés often have whole truffles arranged in a row in the pan so that each slice of pâté contains a slice of truffle. The color contrast of black truffles and white meat is quite eye-catching. Since for us to use a whole row of truffles would be

Our Pâté Maison Bowers is often baked in tiny pans, which make a more festive appearance and somewhat get away from the "meat loaf" connotation.

the same as using a row of gold nuggets, we substitute medium-sized whole mushrooms, which do not provide as good a color contrast with chicken but at least make an appealing design in each slice without costing an arm and a leg.

> 2 lb raw white chicken meat, ground very fine
> 4 egg whites
> 2 tbsp cornstarch
> 2 tbsp sherry
> 1 tsp tarragon extract
> ½ tsp salt
> White pepper, as desired
> Large whole mushrooms

Mix all the ingredients thoroughly and put half into a loaf pan. Arrange the mushrooms standing up in a row down the center of the pan and add the remaining chicken mixture, packing carefully and firmly around the mushrooms. Set the pan in a water bath and bake in a 350-degree oven for 2 hours or until a toothpick comes out clean. Serve sliced, either hot or cold.

TUNA PÂTÉ   *White Grape*

The difference between a spread and a pâté is mainly that the latter can be sliced and will still hold its shape. This means that the pâté must either be made of raw meat which is baked or cooked meat which is set with gelatin. A tuna pâté differs from tuna salad both in texture and in its shape-retaining properties when sliced.

> 2 cans tuna, flaked fine
> 2 tsp grated onion
> 2 tbsp lemon juice
> 1 cup celery, chopped
> ½ cup pimento, chopped
> 2 tbsp sour cream
> 1 tsp curry powder
> 1 envelope unflavored gelatin
> ¼ cup white wine

Soften the envelope of unflavored gelatin in the white wine. Over hot water, heat until the gelatin melts. Add the gelatin to all the ingredients, mix thoroughly, and put into a mold before the gelatin has time to set. Refrigerate and serve on a platter ready for slicing.

VEAL PÂTÉ   *May Wine*

Veal always is a very scrappy meat, quite loosely held together by its own tissues and often needing to be tied with string before cooking. One very good way to use veal scraps, which otherwise are hard to serve, is to shred the cooked orts to go into a gelatin-based pâté.

> **4 cups cold cooked veal, finely shredded with forks**
> **3 or 4 hard-boiled eggs**
> **½ cup each of the following, chopped coarsely: green pepper, celery, pimento, and onion**
> **1 tsp bay leaf extract**
> **1 envelope unflavored gelatin**
> **¼ cup May wine**

Toss all the ingredients except the eggs, gelatin, and wine with the meat. Soften one envelope of unflavored gelatin in ¼ cup of May wine and heat over water until the gelatin is melted. Mix the gelatin with the other ingredients. Put half of the mixture into a loaf pan and arrange the whole hard-boiled eggs in a row down the center. Cover with the remaining mixture and press down around the eggs. Refrigerate until firmly set. At serving time, slice carefully so that the egg slices will remain in place.

TERRINE OF DUCK   *Red Grape*

Most terrines are just a special form of pâté, distinguished by having long slices of some contrasting meat laid in the pan, alternating with a forcemeat base. This is partly to make a pretty slice and partly because a somewhat scarcer meat, whose characteristic appearance should not be destroyed by grinding, is used for the slices. Terrine of duck is an example of this. The duck aspic we speak of is the congealed bouillon we get from boiling the bones and skin with the meat scraps of the bird. This is so firm that it can be sliced.

> **2 lb half-and-half pork and veal, ground very fine**
> **Strips of available duck meat, cooked**
> **Peel of 1 orange, grated fine**
> **½ cup red wine**
> **2 tsp salt (1 tsp per lb of meat)**
> **1 cup duck aspic, or as needed**

Work the salt, duck aspic, and orange peel into the ground meat with about half a cup of red wine. Put a layer of forcemeat into a loaf pan. Make a layer of strips of duck meat and another of forcemeat. Continue in alternate layers, ending with a layer of forcemeat on top. Place in a water bath and bake in a 350-degree oven for 2 hours or until the juices are clear. Cool and then refrigerate before unmolding. Slice with a very sharp knife, carefully so as not to disarrange the duck meat.

LIVERWURST PÂTÉ   *Cabernet*

Liver is not a popular specialty meat with most people. The various forms of liver sausage (wurst), developed largely in Europe, came about for two reasons. First, liver, which deteriorates rapidly, is preserved well in sausage form. Second, the "diluted" liver is better accepted by more people. Many pâté recipes call for ground fresh liver to be added to the standard beef-pork-veal mixture. Fresh liver can be substituted for the prepared liverwurst in our recipe.

> **1 lb standard beef-pork-veal mix, finely ground twice**
> **1 lb liverwurst sausage or fresh liver, finely ground**
> **2 tsp salt**
> **6 juniper berries, crushed fine**
> **1 tsp bay leaf extract**
> **½ tsp ground allspice**
> **½ cup red wine**

Mix all of the ingredients thoroughly and bake in a loaf pan in a water bath at 350 degrees for 2 hours or until the juices are clear. Cool and refrigerate. Best when served cold.

WINE-CHEESE SPREADS

As members of Cheese Lovers International, we consume fantastic amounts of numerous types of cheese, both plain and in combinations. So far, we have made only one kind of spread with cream cheese although any of the wines would be equally tasty. We attempted to emulate that great French cheese, Gourmandise, using a 10-ounce package of cream cheese and adding ½ cup of wild cherry wine with a few drops of almond extract. The texture is a passable facsimile and the subtle cherry-almond flavor is delicious when the mixture is blended thoroughly. We enjoy this on cocktail crackers, storing it in crocks in the refrigerator. It does not freeze well.

Blue cheese seems to call for our sherry wines, either peach, pear, or amoroso. We just crumble the cheese and work in enough wine to give a fairly heavy spread at room temperature, remembering that when fresh from the refrigerator, the spread will be almost too solid. We always get all spreads and pâtés out of the refrigerator about 30 minutes before using. This spread is great on crackers or as a stuffing for celery stalks.

Swiss cheese, other than the processed types, which we never use, is almost too firm to take up wine but by using the fine food grater, we are able to add enough wine to make an excellent spread. The mild fruit wines such as peach, pear, and apple are particularly good although riesling is a good standard choice.

Cheddar cheese is notoriously good with wine and is equally excellent when mixed with wine to make a spread. We use the very sharp cheddar which comes in bricks. Here again we run the cheese through the fine food shredder to make it easier to work. It is quite safe to say that any of the homemade wines are great in spreads with cheddar, but some are outstanding. In particular, quince wine is unbeatable, with strawberry and raspberry coming close seconds and thirds. The other wines follow in less distinguished company. We just work in all the wine the cheese will take, pack it into crocks, and freeze it for later use. Even a good red grape wine makes an excellent spread with cheddar although the muddy purple color may disquiet some stomachs.

Our most superb wine-cheese effort is called simply Cheese Jar and we make it in large quantities because it has multiple uses. It keeps indefinitely in the refrigerator and freezes equally well. To make it, we take one part of very sharp cheddar and one part of imported Swiss cheese, putting them through the fine blade of the food mill. Crumble in a half part, or more if you wish, of blue cheese, mixing the three cheeses and blending in vermouth until a smooth but firm pâté results. This is good on crackers, makes an excellent filling for a brunch omelette, and is delicious when broiled until bubbly on Triscuits. The spread is packed into crocks for freezing until needed later. We have kept a crock going in the refrigerator for at least four years.

Perhaps at this point we should mention that zeal often causes us to buy quite a large piece of cheese, most often, it seems, of the cheddar family, and it tends to dry out before we can eat all of it. This is prevented by wrapping the cheese in cloth or sturdy paper towels, moistened but not dripping with red wine. This not only softens the cheese and improves the flavor but it inhibits any mold from developing. We enclose the wrapped cheese in a plastic bag in the refrigerator.

WINE-CHEESE CROUTONS   *Sherry*

As a pick-up snack with cocktails, try these. Cut a loaf of day-old unsliced white bread into ¾-inch cubes, after removing the crust. This comes out to about 16 cubes per ¾-inch slice. Sprinkle the cubes generously with sherry and then cover them heavily with grated cheese: cheddar, parmesan, romano, or sapsago. Place the cubes on a cooky sheet in a 450-degree oven and turn them over when they are brown on the bottom. This takes about 20 minutes, total, in the oven. Good hot or cold.

Coquilles St. Jacques, baked in individual scallop shells, is a great hot offering on the cocktail buffet table. As an entree, bake en casserole.

COQUILLES ST. JACQUES *Vermouth*

When baked in individual scallop shells or in tiny ramekins, this scallop dish is a delicious hors d'oeuvre or first course. As an entree, it is baked in a large casserole.

> **1 lb scallops**
> **1 cup vermouth**
> **½ cup mushrooms, chopped**
> **1 tbsp parsley, chopped**
> **1 tsp lemon juice**
> **1 small onion or 6 shallots, chopped**
> **2 tbsp butter**
> **2 tbsp flour**
> **1 egg yolk**
> **A little cream**

Cook the scallops in the wine with a bouquet garni and the onion, lemon juice, mushrooms, and parsley, until the scallops are tender. Drain the scallops, cut them into small pieces, and reserve the cooking liquid. Make a roux of the flour and butter, add the stock, and stir until smooth. Beat the egg yolk with a little cream and add some of the hot liquid to it, stirring constantly. Pour the egg mixture into the rest of the hot liquid, continuing to stir constantly to avoid curdling. When thick enough, salt to taste and add the scallops. Spoon the scallop mixture and sauce into individual scallop shells, small ramekins, or one large casserole. Dust the top with crumbs and shredded Swiss cheese. Bake the shells or casserole until bubbly and the cheese is melted, usually not over 20 minutes.

GAZPACHO   *Red Grape*

Do not be misled by the thin tomato juice with some chopped green peppers sprinkled on top, served by most restaurants under the guise of gazpacho. Actually, gazpacho is a very versatile dish which we make in quantity from the products of our garden, freezing it for all-year use. Served frozen, it is a very piquant sherbet-salad with the meal. Thawed, it makes an excellent first course served in glasses as you would serve tomato juice cocktail. Brought to a boil and served as a hot soup, it acquires a quite different and very interesting flavor. Served in very small glasses, it goes well on a buffet table. We will give the recipe for gazpacho in the following chapter on soup.

ITALIAN MEAT BALLS   *Chianti*

Meat balls come in all sizes and in almost all nationalities, with various local additions in taste treats or ingredients to distinguish them. Really, most of the raw pâté mixtures can be cooked as fancy meat balls, if desired. Italian meat balls are distinguished by one or all of the ubiquitous Italian seasonings such as thyme, oregano, basil, and bay leaf. In addition, the Italian variety features a generous addition of grated parmesan cheese, which contributes a pervasive but pleasant odor and taste. We make meat balls in moderate size to serve with pasta or in miniature to go on pizza pie before baking or to be eaten from toothpicks at a pick-up cocktail buffet.

1 lb twice-ground beef-pork-veal mixture
¼ lb Italian sausage, removed from casing and reground
1 cup dry bread crumbs
2 eggs
1 tbsp parsley
½ cup grated parmesan cheese
½ cup chianti
1 onion, chopped
1 tsp salt
½ tsp oregano
½ tsp thyme
½ tsp basil
½ garlic clove, chopped
Generous sprinkling of black pepper

Mix all ingredients thoroughly and make into 1-inch balls. In a skillet, heat equal parts of olive oil and cooking oil. Fry the meat balls with frequent turning, until done. Serve hot with toothpicks or freeze for future use.

SWEDISH MEAT BALLS *Riesling*

The Swedes are famous for their meat balls, usually served in a thick, bubbling-hot sauce. They are a little messy to eat from toothpicks because of the hazards of the sauce, but the sauce is so good that a few dribbles over the chin can be forgiven, especially if everyone else is doing it. The seasoning of Swedish meat balls is the distinguishing feature, depending primarily on the aromatic nutmeg and mace but not necessarily eschewing cinnamon and clove.

2 lb twice-ground beef-pork-veal mixture
1 1-inch slice of day-old white bread, soaked in riesling
2 eggs, beaten
¼ cup chopped onion, sautéed in 1 tbsp butter
3 tbsp chopped parsley
2 tsp salt
Peel of one lemon, grated
1 tsp lemon juice
½ tsp nutmeg
½ tsp mace
½ tsp clove

Mix all the ingredients thoroughly and make into 1-inch balls. Bring to a boil a mixture of 2 cups bouillon and 2 cups riesling. Drop in the meat balls carefully and simmer, covered, for about 15 minutes. Remove the meat and measure the stock. Make a roux of 2 tablespoons butter and 2 tablespoons cornstarch for each cup of stock. Add the roux to the stock and cook until sufficiently thick and the cornstarch has cleared. Add salt and pepper to adjust seasoning. Before serving, heat the meat balls in the gravy and keep hot over a chafing dish. Serve with toothpicks and large napkins.

CAPONATA *Chianti*

Many nations have an eggplant dish, served either hot or cold, used as an hors d'oeuvre or as a main course. One of the best of these is the Italian caponata, which we make in large batches. It can be stored in 2-quart freezer containers in the refrigerator for 3 or 4 months if there is enough vinegar to prevent mold. A large batch can be put in jars, sealed, and processed in a 250-degree oven for 40 minutes. Then it will keep indefinitely on the shelf, but it is too good to last long.

> About 8 cups eggplant, peeled and cut into ½-inch cubes
> Salt
> ½ cup olive oil
> 2 cups chopped celery
> 1 cup chopped onions
> ⅓ cup red vine vinegar and 4 tsp sugar
> ⅓ cup red wine
> 3 cups drained canned tomatoes or fresh tomatoes,
>   chopped and drained
> 2 tbsp tomato paste
> 1 bottle salted dry capers (drain if in vinegar)
> ½ cup sliced stuffed olives
> ½ cup sliced ripe olives, preferably pitted
> Salt and pepper to taste
> ½ cup toasted pine nuts

Sprinkle eggplant cubes generously with salt and set in a colander to drain over the sink for 30 to 40 minutes. Pat the cubes dry with paper towels and set aside. In a heavy skillet, heat ¼ cup oil. Add celery and sauté for 10 minutes, stirring. Add the onions and cook until soft and lightly colored. Transfer to a bowl. Pour the remaining oil into the skillet and, over high heat, sauté the eggplant cubes, stirring constantly for 8 to 10 minutes. Return the celery and onions to the skillet and stir in all but the last two remaining ingredients. Add salt, about 2 teaspoons, and pepper to taste. Simmer uncovered, stirring frequently, for about 15 minutes. Add the pine nuts. Adjust the seasoning with salt and pepper and add more vinegar to taste, if desired.

CHILI CON QUESO *White Grape*

South-of-the-border foods grow more and more popular as increasing numbers of people return home after service at one of the many military installations in the South and Southwest. A favorite cocktail dip, best when served with Fritos or other cornmeal-type dippers, is cheddar cheese, melted to make a pepper-hot chafing dish offering. Processed cheese is best for this purpose, since it melts more easily. Remember that cheese covers up other flavors and it takes a lot of pepper to make this dish, but remember also that the "hot" taste develops slowly. Add-wait-and-taste is the proper procedure.

1 lb processed cheddar cheese
½ cup milk
½ cup white wine (red gives a bad color)
Flour
1 can green hot chilis or cayenne to taste

Melt the cheese with the milk in a double boiler and add the wine. Add shake-in flour, stirring constantly until smooth and dipping-thick. Then add the can of hot chilis, chopped. If preferred, use cayenne or Picante sauce to taste. Serve as a chafing dish specialty. Leftovers can be remelted, broiled on Triscuits, or used as omelette filling.

HOT BEAN DIP   *Zinfandel*

Another good south-of-the-border cocktail buffet dish, fire-hot as well as pepper-hot, is Hot Bean Dip. Bland refried beans customarily are used as fire-quenchers with a Mexican meal, but we like them with pepper-fire added. If canned refried beans with chorizos (Mexican sausage) are available, they add a little more flavor.

> **1 can refried beans with chorizos**
> **¼ cup red wine**
>   **Picante sauce, green hot chilis, or cayenne**
>   **Cheddar cheese (optional)**

Heat the beans and wine in a double boiler and mash the beans to a near-smooth paste. Add your favorite source of pepper-heat, tasting occasionally. Chunks of cheddar cheese melted in the bean mixture make a delicious variation. Serve in a chafing dish.

SCANDINAVIAN SMORREBROD   *May Wine or Sherry*

On a visit to the Scandinavian countries, we were completely captivated by the beautiful, delicious, colorful, endlessly varied open-faced sandwiches which were available everywhere by the trayful for snacks, lunch, brunch, or what not. These works of art and gastronomic delight are simple to make. For example, we use white, rye, pumpernickel, or whole wheat bread. One slice of bread, spread with mayonnaise and covered with lettuce, may hold thin slices of rare leftover beef with rémoulade sauce, topped with tiny sliced tomatoes. Another may be a pumpernickel-ham-Swiss cheese combination with sliced stuffed olives on top. Again, try the mayonnaise-lettuce base for tiny shrimp with mustard dressing and strips of pimento. The various salad mixtures such as tuna, egg, salmon, shrimp, and even potato can be made into dainty and tasty pictures. Any leftover meat such as chicken or pork, decorated with rings of onion and green pepper, makes delicious and attractive surprises. And of course

For brunch, the Scandinavian open-faced sandwiches are elegant, eye-filling, and delicious in a wide variety of ways. Lift to plates with a silver tomato-server and serve with May wine.

any of the pâtés work out well also. Whatever the platter holds, May wine, tarragon or other favorite herb wine, or one of the sherries adds just the right touch, any time of year.

For lunch, brunch, or teatime, use whole slices of bread to make smorrebrod; but for cocktail or buffet snacks, cut the bread into small fancy shapes with a cooky cutter and decorate in miniature with the same selections and combinations of ingredients.

CHAPTER 3

~~~~~~

Soups

The long winter evenings are perfect for a dinner of hearty soup, a great homemade dry wine, a delicious appropriate bread, a delightful tossed salad, cheese and fruit with coffee and a homemade liqueur. The only possible improvement is candlelight, a sympathetic companion, and a soup made with your own wine. Actually, with an air-conditioned house, the changing seasons make little difference in our eating habits and we have hearty soups frequently, throughout the year. We have many favorites which alternate with the perpetual soup pot or with the plastic containers labeled "For Soup," stored in the freezer. Soups are not as popular for main dishes in America as they are in some European countries, but with a little resourcefulness and persistence, this economical taste can be acquired with pleasurable results.

PHILADELPHIA
MOCK SNAPPER SOUP   *Pear Sherry*

For many years, a highlight of any visit to Philadelphia had to be a bowl of the famous snapper soup at Bookbinder's Restaurant. Several years ago, while on a visit there, we were greatly impressed with this justly celebrated soup. We talked about this for some years, trying to come up with a good, available, economical substitute for the firm bits of turtle meat. We finally found such a substitute in chicken hearts, which have just the right consistency and do not have too distinctive a flavor of their own. Thus we devised our Philadelphia Mock Snapper Soup and here it is.

2 lb chicken hearts with fat and large vessels trimmed off, each cut into 2-3 pieces
1 cup flour
1 tsp salt
½ tsp black pepper
½ lb salt pork, cut into ¼ -inch dice
1½ cups chopped onion
1 cup chopped celery
½ cup chopped carrot
½ tsp garlic chips
1 qt beef or chicken bouillon
2 tbsp tomato paste
1 tsp bay leaf extract
½ tsp thyme
3 tbsp pear sherry

Pat the cut-up hearts dry on a paper towel and shake them in a plastic bag with the flour, salt, and pepper. In a heavy skillet, over moderate heat, fry the fat pork cubes until crisp and brown, with all fat rendered. Drain the dice on paper towels and set aside.

Brown the hearts in several batches in the pork fat, until richly colored. Pour off all but about 3 tablespoons of fat and add the onion, celery, carrot, and garlic. Sauté this mirepoix

Philadelphia Mock Snapper Soup with pear sherry is a hearty dish. With a hard roll and a tossed salad, nothing more is needed except pleasant companionship.

over moderate heat until soft but not brown. Stir in the stock, tomato paste, herbs, and pork dice. Bring to a boil and add the hearts with any accumulated juices. Reduce heat and simmer, partially covered, for 2 hours. Replace liquid with stock if it boils away too rapidly. Add about 1 tablespoon pear sherry to each soup plate just before serving with French or Italian bread. This marvelous, hearty soup, like most stews, actually improves with reheating.

BORSCHT   *Zinfandel*

Borscht, depending on the country and region of origin, can be anything from watery boiled cabbage or beets to a sumptuous repast. Our version is modeled somewhat after the Ukrainian style and, because we grow kohlrabi, we substituted it for the more plebeian and "dribbly" cabbage. This soup, like many soups and stews, seems to get better every time it is warmed up.

1 pt canned tomatoes
1 cup chopped onions
1 lb shredded beets
1 cup red grape wine
2 qt beef stock
1 lb kohlrabi, shredded
½ pt sour cream
4 tbsp butter
2 cloves chopped garlic
¼ cup chopped parsley
1 tbsp salt
1 lb diced raw potatoes
1½ lb cubed beef brisket

Brown the meat in the butter in a casserole and then add the wine and stock. Simmer for about an hour or until the meat is

Ukrainian-style borscht does well with shredded kohlrabi instead of the usual soggy cabbage leaves.

tender. Add all the remaining ingredients except the sour cream and simmer for another 40 minutes. Adjust the seasoning and put a large dollop of sour cream in each dish just before bringing it to the table. Serve with the blackest bread you can bake or buy.

SEAFOOD BISQUE   *Vermouth*

Seafood bisque is a most versatile dish and can really be a never-twice-the-same surprise, because you can use lobster, shrimp, scallops, clams, crab, fish chunks, or any combination of these or the more exotic sea creatures, if you care for them.

        1½ lb seafood, prepared for cooking
         2 qt beef or chicken stock
         6 tbsp brown roux
         1 cup chopped celery
         2 tbsp chopped garlic
         1 1-lb can tomatoes
         1 tbsp tomato paste
         1 tsp cayenne
         2 cups chopped onions
         ¼ cup chopped parsley
         1 tsp bay leaf extract
         ¼ tsp thyme
         ½ tsp black pepper
        1½ tsp salt
         3 tbsp vermouth
           Pear sherry

Put all the seafood through the fine blade of the food grinder. There should be about 3 cups of the meat. Brown 6 tablespoons of flour in vegetable oil to make the brown roux and add all the vegetables, cooking until soft, about 5 minutes. Add the seafood and all the other ingredients, stirring in the stock over low heat. Simmer for 45 minutes. Put the bisque in the blender and whirl until smooth. Reheat the bisque carefully, adjust the seasoning, and add 1 tablespoon pear sherry to each dish just before serving with French or Italian bread.

GUMBO   *Chenin Blanc*

Creole soups and stews often call for file gumbo, a ropy thickening agent made from the leaves or root bark of the sassafras tree. We have been quite intrigued by this but neither the boughten file gumbo nor our own product of pulverized dried sassafras leaves does anything but flavor the dish rather delightfully while contributing to a muddy color. We now just settle for the flavor and forget the thickening. Our gumbo is excellent if not exactly traditional. The okra itself contributes a mucilaginous quality, and this is as close as we can get.

1 lb medium uncooked shrimp
3 qt bouillon
2 tsp crushed red peppers
1 lemon, thinly sliced
1 tsp bay leaf extract
1 tsp thyme
1 tbsp salt
3 tbsp brown roux
½ cup onion, coarsely chopped
2 tsp garlic, finely chopped
½ lb okra, in 1-inch lengths
¾ cup green pepper, coarsely chopped
1 tsp cayenne
½ tsp Tabasco
1 tbsp file gumbo powder
1 pt white wine
6 cups freshly cooked long-grain rice

Shell and devein the shrimp. Boil the shrimp in the bouillon and wine until pink. Remove and reserve the stock with the shrimp. Make a brown roux of flour and butter, half and half, and in this, sauté the onion, garlic, okra, and green pepper. Add the shrimp and slowly pour in the reserved stock, adding all the seasonings except the file gumbo, stirring constantly. Simmer for about an hour and, after the heat is turned off, add the file gumbo, stirring well. Adjust for salt and cayenne.

To serve, put a large scoop of the cooked rice in each heated soup plate and spoon the gumbo around and over it.

FRUIT SOUP

Apple Wine

The fruit soups are primarily Scandinavian in origin and lend themselves to endless variation, according to personal whim and availability of ingredients. Many of the fruit soups depend on cherries, both red and black, but with many apples and many gallons of apple wine, we devised the following.

In a saucepan, stir 1½ tablespoons of quick-cooking tapioca into ¾ cup of boiling water. Cook the tapioca, stirring constantly, until the mixture is clear. Now stir in 1½ cups each of grape juice and apple wine, ¼ cup of sugar, 2 tablespoons of grated lemon rind, and ¼ teaspoon of ground cinnamon. Cook over low heat, stirring constantly for 10 minutes, and let cool. Stir in 2 cups of apple sauce, ¼ cup of sour cream, and ¼ cup of cherry brandy. Whip until smooth and pour into a tureen. Chill for 4 hours, covered. Serve sprinkled with grated nutmeg and garnished with floating apple slices. This is just a beginning and should suggest endless possibilities for delectable fruit soup combinations.

Fruit Soup in this instance shows the color of grape juice, although it is made with apple wine as well, but any other juice such as cherry or cranberry makes a good variant. The cross-section of uncored apple adds a nice touch with its pretty star pattern.

Gazpacho is excellent in any of three forms. In the compote dish is gaz-pacho frozen to a firm mush, being served as a frozen salad. Being poured from the blender is gazpacho as it is served as a first course or a buffet table cocktail. In the soup dish is hot gazpacho, decorated with cucumber, onion, and green pepper.

GAZPACHO SOUP   *Chianti*

We have discussed gazpacho as a frozen salad and as a tomato cocktail-like drink (see chapter 2), but here we stress it as a hot soup. The recipe is the same for use in any of these ways.

> 2 tbsp olive oil
> ⅛ tsp garlic chips
> ¼ cup red wine
> 1 carrot
> ½ cucumber
> 1 stalk celery
> ½ green pepper
> 1 tsp salt
> 1 small onion
> ¼ tsp powdered cayenne
> 3 large ripe tomatoes

Chop the vegetables finely and put all the ingredients into a 5-cup blender. Blend at high speed, adding more tomato if needed to make the jar full after blending. Package for freezing, if the soup is not to be used at once.

CUCUMBER BISQUE   *Riesling*

Our cucumber bisque originated by accident or by serendipity, as so many things do. We were faced with a bumper crop of cucumbers and despite voracious eating of raw cucumbers at cocktail time, numerous Chinese salads of thin-sliced cucumbers in vinegar with toasted sesame seeds, and other usages, we were being inundated. Casting about for a solution, we developed cucumber bisque. As a result, we froze blended cucumber concentrate in pint containers, each of which makes one batch of bisque with the addition of milk. Now, we can have cucumber bisque all year long whenever the spirit moves us.

> 3 large cucumbers
> ¼ cup onion, chopped fine
> 3 tbsp butter
> 3 tbsp flour
> 3 cups bouillon
> 1½ cups milk
> ½ cup instant mashed potatoes
> ½ cup white wine
> Salt and pepper
> Chopped chives or tarragon

Peel the cucumbers, section lengthwise, and remove the seeds. Sauté the cucumber and onion in the butter for about 10 minutes. Stir in the flour and then add the chicken bouillon, stirring constantly. Add the milk and simmer for 10 minutes. Add the instant mashed potatoes and blend at high speed until smooth. Stir in the white wine. Add salt and pepper to taste. Serve thoroughly chilled with chopped fresh chives or tarragon on top.

To freeze, stop at the point before adding the milk. The remaining preparations are made after thawing for use. Reblend to restore the smooth texture.

CHEDDAR CHEESE SOUP   *Red Grape Wine*

This is a hearty soup, more suited for a brunch or Sunday night supper than as a first course at dinner. The color combinations are pleasing and the soup is delicious.

> ½ **tsp cayenne**
> ½ **cup chopped green peppers**
> 4 **tbsp butter**
> ½ **cup minced celery**
> ½ **cup minced onion**
> ½ **cup chopped chives**
> 3 **garlic cloves, chopped fine**
> 4 **tbsp flour**
> ½ **cup red grape wine**
> 1 **qt milk**
> 1 **lb very sharp cheddar, grated**
> **Salt**

Sauté all the vegetables except the chives in the butter until lightly browned. Sprinkle with the flour, cook slowly, and add the wine, stirring until smooth. Over low heat, add the milk and then the cheese, stirring until the cheese melts and the soup is smooth. Season with salt and cayenne and serve sprinkled with the chopped chives.

VICHYSOISSE   *Pear Sherry*

Vichysoisse is simply potato soup fancied up a little bit and served cold. We just carried the evolution a step further by adding a filip of pear sherry. The lazy way to make this soup is to use instant mashed potato powder to obviate all the peeling, slicing, cooking, and blending.

Sauté 1 medium onion in 2 tablespoons of butter until soft and beginning to brown. Then add 4 potatoes, peeled and sliced thin. Add a pint of bouillon and cook until the potatoes disintegrate. Salt to taste and blend until smooth. Cool. Add 1 cup of milk and a cup of medium cream with ½ cup of white wine. Chill thoroughly and serve with chopped chives on top.

CHAPTER 4

~~~~~~

Beef

"**B**eef and potato man" always has been a rather disparaging and snobbish way of describing a gentleman who is a prosaic, plodding sort of fellow with little flair for the dramatic and lacking in imagination. Further, the British, never known for their culinary skills, have been regarded as the champions of roast beef as their only gastronomic claim to fame. As with all stereotypes, these are inaccurate. There are hundreds of ways of preparing beef dishes, many of which literally are fit for a king, of whatever country. Many of our most highly favored recipes are based on beef, especially if cooked with wines.

ONION SOUP BEEF ROAST   *Red Grape Wine*

For those who like their beef well done, this, in our opinion,

Onion Soup Beef Roast is a well-done preparation which, if possible, is better in its many leftover guises than it is as a hot roast.

is the world's best recipe. Not only is it delightful the first time around but the serendipitous side results are outstanding.

We prefer a 4- or 5-pound bottom round beef roast, but rump or any boneless potroast cut is suitable. The roast is placed in the center of a large sheet of heavy-duty foil, and over the meat is sprinkled one whole envelope of Lipton's onion soup mix. Then, around the roast we pour two or more cups of dry red grape wine. The foil is tightly sealed by a druggist's fold across the top and double folds at each end. The roast is placed in a preheated 300-degree oven and cooked for 5-6 hours. Even a frozen roast can be cooked in this way without prior thawing. It is best to let the cooked roast rest for about 15 minutes before slicing it; even then, the electric knife works best.

The pan juices from the roast make an excellent thickened gravy with potatoes, rice, noodles, or biscuits. We always reserve some juice and even the leftover gravy to add to the perpetual soup pot. Slices of the roast heated in the gravy make tasty hot roast beef sandwiches. When cold, the roast can be sliced thin and makes an excellent cold plate or open-faced sandwich in the Scandinavian manner with mustard, mayonnaise, or rémoulade sauce. The really outstanding use for the leftover roast is a variety of sauerbraten. For this, we make ½- to ¾-inch-thick slices of beef and moisten each with about a teaspoon of vinegar, letting the meat marinate for an hour. Then salt and pepper and dip each slice in beaten egg and cornflake crumbs. Pan-fry to a deep brown and serve immediately with chili sauce. Of all the well-done beef roasts, this one is our favorite for aroma, flavor, good eating, and culinary bonuses.

BEEF ROULADES   *Zinfandel*

A roulade is a roll. Beef rolls are known as *roulades* in France, *Rouladen* in Germany, and *rollatini* in Italy. With a wide variety of stuffings and under whatever name, roulades are one of our most cherished treats.

A roulade usually consists of a piece of meat with special filling. Even rolled boned veal or pork roasts can be so designated. Probably the world's largest roulade is made by the Argentinians, who lay out a whole flank steak, cover it with various vegetables, roll and tie it, roast it, and serve it in slices. Since any rolled item can properly be called a roulade, we should include such special forms as the banana leaf rolls of the tropics, the grape leaf rolls of many Near East countries, and the cabbage leaf rolls of the north European Slavs.

For Beef Roulades, have the butcher cut very thin slices of top round from the larger end and pound each piece even thinner between sheets of butcher paper. Plan 1 large or 2 small roulades per person.

Large thin slices of top round
Hot sausage (pepper-hot)
Onion, chopped fine
Parsley, chopped
Salt and black pepper
Flour for dredging
Red grape wine

To assemble the roulades, spread out a sheet of the beef and sprinkle it with salt and pepper. Then spread it thickly with a layer of your favorite pepper-hot sausage. Over this, sprinkle a good layer of the finely chopped onion and chopped parsley. Tightly roll each piece of beef around its stuffing and tie it securely in several places with heavy string. Roulades may be frozen at this point for subsequent use.

To cook, dredge each roulade in flour and brown nicely on all sides in hot oil in a casserole. Pour a hearty red wine over the roulades, using about half a cup per roulade or enough to half cover them in the casserole. Bake covered in a preheated 325-degree oven for 2 hours or until the meat is well done. Cut and remove the strings carefully. Arrange the roulades on a heated platter and serve the pan juices separately, or slightly thicken with flour and pour the sauce over the roulades. The cooked roulades freeze well and heat up beautifully.

Beef Roulades stuffed with hot sausage and chopped onion have a peasant look but are of gourmet caliber in aroma and taste.

Shown here are the principal ingredients of Beef Catalan. Beef Catalan and most other dishes should have all of the ingredients assembled first not only to be sure that you have everything you need but to get first things done first.

BEEF CATALAN   *Tea Wine*

Almost every country has several delectable stews in its cuisine and with just a subtle change of seasonings, a whole new dish emerges. Beef Catalan is a good example with its unusual use of white wine. Its saffron and parmesan cheese strongly bespeak a southern European origin.

    2 lb lean stewing beef, in 1-inch cubes
    2 cups sliced onions
    ½ tsp minced garlic
    1 pt canned tomatoes
    5 medium potatoes, peeled and cut in ¼ -inch slices
    ½ tsp thyme
    1 tsp bay leaf extract
    1 good pinch of saffron
      Parmesan cheese, grated
    1 cup bouillon
    1 cup tea wine

Brown the meat in oil, remove from the pan, and reserve. Brown the onions and garlic, remove from the pan, and reserve.

Beef Catalan is served directly from its oven casserole. Sliced potatoes form the top layer.

In an oven casserole, arrange the meat with the onions and garlic on top. Separately heat the bouillon and spices with the wine. Pour the tomatoes over the meat. Fill the casserole almost to the top of the meat and tomatoes with the wine-bouillon-spice mixture. Make an overlapping layer of potato slices on top. Cook covered for 2-3 hours in a 325-degree preheated oven. Half an hour before serving time, remove the casserole lid, sprinkle on a thick layer of grated parmesan cheese, and con-

Stews such as Beef Catalan need to be served on heated plates because they cool so rapidly.

tinue cooking for half an hour, uncovered. Serve with crusty white bread and a tossed salad. A glass of wine is all that is needed to complete a perfect, hearty meal. Beef Catalan reheats or freezes beautifully.

Boeuf Bourguignon is almost the only dish we know which does not contain any herbs and spices. Onions, carrots, meat, and wine carry the dish to great heights with no outside help.

BOEUF BOURGUIGNON   *Cabernet*

Fortunately, this classic French stew is known by its French name and is never, but never, called a "stew." Every nation has some outstandingly good stews, but the name "stew" seems to connote some plebeian mediocrity which could not possibly be very elegant. Boeuf Bourguignon is terrible to spell correctly, but it is so delicious that all is forgiven.

Dredge well in flour 2 or 3 pounds of lean beef, cut into 1- to 1½-inch cubes. Brown the meat on all sides in a mixture of butter and oil. Add 1 cup beef bouillon and 1 cup red wine, and simmer for about 3 hours. Thirty minutes before serving time, adjust seasoning and add 1 8½-ounce can of small whole potatoes, 1 6-ounce can of sliced mushrooms, 1 16-ounce jar small white onions, and 1 16-ounce can baby carrots. When heated through, thicken with flour, to the desired consistency. Serve with hot French or Italian hard rolls. If fresh mushrooms are used, sauté them in butter first. Note that this recipe does not contain any herbs.

BEEF BARCELONA   *Chianti*

Tomatoes, olives, peppers, and orange give this roast of beef a very South European flair with an unusual flavor.

    ¼ **tsp marjoram**
    ¼ **tsp black pepper**
    ¼ **tsp ground clove**
    1 **clove garlic, crushed**
    1 **4- to 5-pound beef potroast**
    ¾ **cup chopped onion**
    1 **cup chianti**
      Peel of 1 orange, grated
    1 **cup stuffed olives**
    ¾ **tsp salt**
    1 **tsp ground cinnamon**
    1 **tbsp chopped parsley**
    4 **tbsp olive oil**
    1 **chopped green pepper**
    1 **lb canned tomatoes**
    ½ **cup orange juice**
    1 **tbsp cornstarch**

Blend all the seasonings, including the orange peel, in half the olive oil and rub this well into the roast; then let the meat stand at room temperature for at least an hour to absorb the flavors. Brown the meat nicely on all sides in the remaining olive oil. Remove and reserve. Sauté the onion and green pepper in the oil until tender. Return the meat and add the tomatoes, wine, and orange juice. Bring to a boil and simmer 3-4 hours or until the meat is tender. If preferred, roast the preparation in a 325-degree oven, basting occasionally. Remove the roast to a heated

Here the beef for Beef Barcelona soaks in its marinade of olive oil and seasonings. It is surrounded by the other principal ingredients for later addition.

platter. Mix the cornstarch with a little extra wine and stir into the pan juices, letting the sauce simmer about 5 minutes and stirring in the stuffed olives.

BRAISED TENDERLOIN TIPS   *Red Grape Wine*

The contrast between European and American cuisine is nowhere more apparent than in the serving of meat. Americans go for cooking whole hams, entire filets, huge thick steaks, and everything on the grand scale; whereas the Europeans settle for small pieces of meat, not necessarily the bite-sized pieces favored by orientals, but what we think of as small. The use of small pieces of beef permits wider use of the chafing dish for tableside preparation. One excellent such recipe is for braised tenderloin tips with mushrooms in wine sauce.

1 lb thin tenderloin tip slices
1½ cups fresh mushrooms, sliced, or 1 6-oz can button
    mushrooms
2 tbsp cooking oil
4 tbsp butter
2 tbsp chopped shallots
¾ cup red wine
1 beef bouillon cube
Cornstarch

Sauté the shallots and mushrooms in 2 tablespoons butter and 2 tablespoons oil. Add the red wine and the bouillon cube, simmering to reduce the volume to about half a cup. Add sufficient cornstarch to thicken wine mixture. In a chafing dish, melt 2 tablespoons butter and sauté the beef until brown but not well done. Add the shallot-mushroom-wine sauce and heat thoroughly. Serve with French or Italian hard rolls or over rice or noodles.

A quick, easy, and delicious chafing-dish specialty is Braised Tenderloin Tips with slivers of tender meat which do not need either high heat or long cooking.

BEEF STROGANOFF

Zinfandel

Beef Stroganoff was originated as a chafing dish specialty to be cooked at tableside with flair and verve, using quick-cooking morsels of tenderloin tip. An unavowed goal probably was to stretch a small quantity of scrappy pieces as far as possible but no matter; the end result is delicious and fancy. We have modified the recipe somewhat, often using thin strips of leftover rare london broil. Although the dish is traditionally served over noodles, we sometimes use spaetzle or some other form of pasta and have even been guilty of serving it over fluffy rice.

> ½ lb tenderloin tips in thin short pieces
> About 2 tbsp butter
> ½ cup sliced onions
> 1 cup sliced mushrooms, preferably fresh
> ½ cup beef bouillon
> ½ cup red wine
> 4 tbsp sour cream
> 2 dashes nutmeg
> Salt and pepper

Salt and pepper the meat and brown it in butter, in a chafing dish at the table, if desired. Add the onions and continue to sauté until they begin to brown. Add the mushrooms and turn until they give up their moisture. Add the bouillon and wine, simmering for 5 minutes. Lower the heat, sprinkle on the nutmeg, and stir in the sour cream. Keep the dish hot but do not boil after adding the sour cream. Serve on heated plates over noodles, spaetzle, or fluffy rice. For a delicious variation, substitute large, uncooked, deveined shrimp for the beef, a white wine for the red, and chicken bouillon for the beef bouillon. Serve in the same way or over toast points.

STUFFED FLANK STEAK

Burgundy

Using a whole flank steak, trim it well, sprinkle with salt and pepper, fold it in the center, and sew the three edges, leaving only enough opening to permit spooning in the stuffing, which is made with the following:

> ½ **cup packed bread crumbs**
> ½ **cup milk**
> ½ **cup red wine**
> 1 **onion, chopped**
> ½ **cup chopped mushrooms**
> 1 **egg**
>   **Salt and pepper**
>   **A few dashes of allspice and nutmeg**

Mix all the ingredients thoroughly and fill the steak pocket with this stuffing. Close the opening with a skewer or more stitches of twine. Place the stuffed steak in a deep pan and half cover with red wine. Braise for 2 hours in a 350-degree oven. Remove the meat to a heated platter and while it is resting, thicken the pan juices with 2 tablespoons of cornstarch in a little wine. Add mushrooms to this sauce, if desired. Serve the sauce separately or over the meat, which is served sliced.

Stuffed Flank Steak makes an intriguing dish when sliced. The sour cream biscuits add a voluptuous touch.

The Beef-stuffed Green Peppers were left with their lids off here to show the very homogeneous consistency of the forcemeat. Extra stuffing is baked separately.

BEEF-STUFFED GREEN PEPPERS   *Chianti*

Green peppers may be stuffed with a raw meat mixture, but for us this recipe serves as one of many uses for leftover cooked beef. Even leftovers of beef from the hickory-smoke grill are excellent here, whereas for most other purposes the smoky taste gets in the way.

> 4 large green peppers
> 3 cups ground leftover beef
> 1½ cups mashed potatoes
> ½ cup chopped onion
> ½ cup red wine
> 1 tbsp Angostura bitters
> 2 tbsp your favorite hot sauce
> ¼ tsp ground allspice
> Salt and pepper

Remove caps from the peppers with a sharp knife; cut out the cores and seeds, reserving the "lids." Mix remaining ingredients thoroughly, taste for seasoning, and fill the peppers with this stuffing. Press the lids in place and set the peppers in a baking dish so that they will stand upright. Bake in a 350-degree oven, covered, for 40-45 minutes.

SUKIYAKI   *Rice Wine*

Having lived three years in Japan, we became very interested in Japanese cooking. Since the main dish in a Japanese dinner contains rice wine and since rice wine is consumed all during the meal, we feel justified in giving you a full Japanese menu rather than the recipe for a single dish. A typical Japanese menu which you can prepare with ease in an authentic manner includes rice wine, roasted peanuts, dried squid, sukiyaki, chawan mushi, tempura, pickles, rice, fruit, and green tea. Ingredients for most of these dishes are available canned; they may also be obtained fresh in any good Chinese store in our larger cities, but such shopping requires a lot of pointing and describing because the Chinese merchants do not know the Japanese names.

The Japanese table is set with many small bowls and saucers instead of dinner plates, with the *hibachi* (charcoal brazier) in front of the host. We substitute a 2-burner electric plate and since dinner is cooked at the table, the seated guests have at least a 30-minute waiting period to enjoy the hot rice wine (*sake*) or green tea (*ocha*) and the hors d'oeuvres. The green tea, served very hot in covered mugs, is sipped noisily without cream or sugar. To most Americans this tastes and smells like an infusion of poor-grade hay; so you may prefer the hot rice wine, served in thimble-sized cups. Serve it throughout the meal if you wish. The unsalted peanuts (*nankimame*), roasted in their brown husks, are munched with the dried squid (*ika*). To prepare this, generously sprinkle salt on the whole dried squid and toast it over a hot burner. When pliable and still hot, it can be torn crosswise with the fingers into narrow strips (*surume*), which are salty, chewy, fishy, and excellent with cocktails. You may prefer an assortment of rice flour crackers (*osembei*).

During the preliminary munching, the host is cooking the sukiyaki (pronounced skee-yah-kee) over the burner before him. Two round cake pans about 2 inches deep will serve 8 people. Into each pan, place a tablespoon of oil (*abura*), 3 ounces of soy sauce (*shoyu*), 3 ounces of rice wine or other white wine, and a teaspoon of sugar (*sato*). From large platters at the side, which the hostess has slaved over for hours, add the various ingredients with additional oil, soy sauce, and wine as needed. The meat is beef (*gyuniku*) or chicken (*toriniku*), cut into thin bite-sized slivers. The platters are heaped with sliced large green onions, really leeks (*negi*); sliced mushrooms (*kinoko*), either dried, fresh, or canned; a vegetable noodle (*konnyaku*), which the Chinese merchant knows as "long rice"; bamboo shoots (*takenoko*), fresh or, preferably, canned; bean curd (*tofu*), cut into cubes, and Chinese water chestnuts or, if available, lotus root (*renkon*). All ingredients are sliced or cubed into bite-sized pieces except the *konnyaku*, which is soaked or precooked like pasta, which it somewhat resembles. *Please*, no green beans, carrots, spinach, cabbage, or other misguided additions which may make a good stew but certainly not sukiyaki. Some of all the ingredients are added to both pans and cooked about 20 minutes, until the onions are done, until the other things are hot and have absorbed the delicious combined flavors, or until the guests (*okya kusama*) will not wait a moment longer. Fill each guest's small plate and then refill the pans so that the cooking is continuous. In Japan, what remains after all are satiated goes to the family and servants, drooling in the kitchen, awaiting their turn. You will want to warm up these leftovers on another day when they will taste even better. One little bowl before each guest contains a raw egg (*tomago*), beaten until frothy; into this, the sukiyaki is dipped very hot and then eaten.

Chawan mushi, a kind of seafood custard, served either before the sukiyaki or with it, is made in a covered Japanese teacup (*chanomi jawan*), which really is a mug. A custard cup may be substituted. Into each cup place bits of precooked beef, veal, chicken, shrimp (*ebi*), or fish (*sakana*); slices of mushrooms, and pieces of lotus root or tender young fern fiddles. If neither of the last two items is available, substitute a raw spinach leaf (*horenso*) or some watercress. Fill the cup with meat or fish stock containing enough raw egg so that a firm custard will form when the whole dish is cooked in a pan of boiling water (*oyu*). Obviously not a chopstick (*hashi*) dish, chawan mushi is eaten with a porcelain spoon (*saji*).

Tempura, the next course, is prepared by the hostess and permits great variety because anything dipped in batter and deep fat-fried is tempura. The Japanese use sesame seed oil (*goma abura*), but any cooking oil will do with your favorite batter. The tempura plates might contain large prawns (*ebi*), whole mushrooms, onion rings, and slices of sweet potato (*satsumaimo*). A trilobed green leaf (*mitsuba*) is not available here, but we have discovered that sprigs of watercress make a wonderful substitute. Canned squid is excellent as are Irish potatoes (*jagaimo*), eggplant (*nasu*), squash (*kabocha*), and carrots (*ninjin*). Two of the little bowls in front of each guest contain soy sauce and horseradish *(wasabi),* which each mixes to taste as a dip for the tempura pieces.

By this time most North Americans will have dined sufficiently, but at this point the Japanese serve heaping bowls of boiled rice (*gohan*). Served earlier, with a spoonful of sukiyaki juice, it is delicious. Any Japanese meal, even breakfast, ends with soup (*suimono*). The simplest is water with salt (*shio*), pepper (*kosho*), and a little butter (*bata*), in which small clams (*hamaguri*) have been cooked. A few clams left in the lacquered soup bowl (*owan*) make a pretty picture. The most universal Japanese soup is miso shiru, made by adding a tablespoon of fermented red bean paste to each bowl of soup. This soup offends some North Americans because of its slight hydrogen sulfide odor, but the flavor is marvelous. Another easy soup contains small pieces of scallop, watercress, and onion. At a really pretentious Japanese dinner, two soups may be served, one midway through the meal and the other at the end.

Just as soup finishes every Japanese meal, so pickles (*tsukemono*) accompany every meal, even breakfast. These pickles usually are salty rather than sour and often contain horseradish or mustard *(karashi).* Chinese cabbage *(hakusai)* may be pickled, but the favorite is *daikon,* a huge white radish which looks and tastes like a turnip. For our dinner, the best substitute is cucumber *(kyuri),* sliced as thin as possible and served in ice-cold water *(kori mizu)* containing vinegar *(su),* salt and a little sugar. These pickles go in one of the little individual bowls.

Dessert after a Japanese meal is not necessary, but fresh fruit *(kudamono)* such as pear *(nashi),* peach *(momo),* persimmon *(kaki),* tangerine *(mikan),* watermelon *(suika),* or grapes *(budo)* is typical, in season.

Such a repast *(shokuji)* is typically Japanese, is not difficult to prepare, and will send your knowledgeable guests away murmuring the polite phrase, *"Go chiso sama deshita"* ("You went to a lot of trouble to prepare this delicious meal!"), to which you reply with a humble bow and suitable modesty, *"Do itashimashite"* ("It was my pleasure").

CHILI CON CARNE
Y FRIJOLES   *Red Grape Wine*

Few dishes arouse more red-hot controversy than chili. Should it be really hot or just almost hot? Should you grind the meat or use chunks? Add the beans or serve them as a side dish? Make it thin like a soup or thick like a stew? Well, we leave the arguers to their verbal battles and meantime, here is how we do it.

> **2 lb well-trimmed beef in ½-inch cubes**
> **2 cans undiluted beef bouillon**
> **1 cup red wine**
> **1 cup chopped onion**
> **4 tbsp chili powder (more if you can take it)**
> **2 1-lb cans pinto beans**
> **salt**

Bring the bouillon and wine to a boil and add the meat chunks. Simmer covered until the meat is tender. Remove the scum which accumulates. Mix the onion and chili powder together and add to the pot. Cook until the meat has absorbed flavor and the onions are done. Check seasoning at this point and add more chili powder, if needed. Add the beans and cook until all are hot but not until they become mushy. With this, we

Chili con Carne y Frijoles is served in a soup plate. The salad is a Mexican-style taco and the "roll" is a variety of nacho with refried bean spread, cheese, and hot sauce.

like corn bread; even better is a species of nachos. Split hot-dog rolls lengthwise and spread with a thick layer of mashed refried beans. Sprinkle with a little chopped onion and a good coating of shredded cheddar cheese. Dribble your favorite hot sauce liberally over the bean filling and put the rolls into the oven until they are hot and the cheese is bubbly.

To complete the chili supper, you might as well make the Mexican salad as well. Fold tortillas in the center loosely and crisp them by brief frying in hot oil. Drain on paper towels. Make a mixture of shredded lettuce, tomato chunks, chopped onion, and shredded cheddar cheese. Add some mashed avocado or use the canned avocado puree *(guacamole)*. Stuff the mixture into the folded tortillas and drizzle over all a heavy sauce made by diluting mashed refried beans with your favorite hot sauce. These concoctions are called tacos. Try orange-chocolate liqueur (see chapter 17) in your coffee for dessert.

LONDON BROIL   *Red Wine*

There are two very separate dishes, both of which are called london broil and both of which are excellent. A very easy method of preparation uses a piece of top round cut so that one chunk is an individual serving. Marinate the pieces in red wine for an hour or so and pat dry. Broil the pieces in the oven or over a hickory-smoke grill, leaving the meat well seared on the outside but red on the inside. Serve on heated plates and let each diner carve his own chunk into bite-size pieces. Have salt and pepper as well as hot sauce available.

The other method uses flank steak which is cut crosswise into 1-inch strips. Marinate the strips in red wine for an hour or so and tumble-dry in a paper towel. Roll each strip tightly and secure it with a bamboo sliver or skewer. Set the pinwheels on edge in a pan and put a dot of butter in each roll. Broil for about 2 minutes and then turn for about 2 minutes on the other edge. If you wish, make miniature roulades of these by stuffing a shrimp into the end of each pinwheel before broiling. Serve with french-fried potatoes and onion rings in beer batter.

By the way, beer batter is useful for anything which is deep- or pan-fried. We use the recipe of our late friend, Chef Albert

Pinwheel-style London Broil of flank steak is held in shape by slivers of bamboo; each pinwheel contains a dot of butter. These will be broiled in the oven rather than over the grill.

After broiling the London Broil pinwheels for three minutes or less on each side, serve them with French-fried potatoes and onion rings. Various wine sauces accompany this dinner.

Stockli, formerly of New York's Four Seasons Restaurant and his own kitchen at Stonehenge Inn, Ridgefield, Connecticut. Pour a 12-ounce can of beer into a mixing bowl. Sift in 1 cup of all-purpose flour, 1 tablespoon of salt, and 1 tablespoon of paprika. Whisk until light and frothy. This batter will keep for a week or so in the refrigerator or freezes well for later use. Just whisk to reconstitute before using.

IMPERIAL MEAT LOAF   *Red Grape Wine*

We coined the fancy title just to distinguish between meat loaf with wine poured around it and meat loaf with wine worked into it. You may use the method with your favorite meat loaf recipe, remembering that the more material such as bread crumbs, the more wine that can be soaked up. It is difficult to get straight ground meat to take up much liquid but you can work in at least half a cup of red wine per two pounds of meat. With crumb or cereal fillers, at least twice as much will go in. This method is excellent, whatever meat is used, being especially good with ham loaf. Just work in what the meat will take. Whatever boils out in the cooking simply adds to the delicious pan juices. The only problem is that the wine-meat loaf is rather fluffy and difficult to slice when hot. Cold, it is no problem.

Imperial Meat Loaf is soft and fluffy with its content of red wine. The onions and green peppers are added for eye-appeal.

SOUR CREAM SWISS STEAK   *Zinfandel*

Where the Swiss get into this we do not know, because the sour cream dishes tend to be Russian-Polish-Czech and/or Jewish. The Austrians also use sour cream and since Austria is a neighbor of Switzerland, maybe propinquity did it. In most of the sour cream recipes, the sour cream is added late and not boiled with the rest of the ingredients. For this reason, wine can be used with the sour cream dishes because the alcohol has evaporated before the sour cream is added. The Swiss steak method is a good means of tenderizing an otherwise somewhat difficult cut of meat.

> 2 lb Swiss steak in serving-size pieces
> 1 tsp salt
> ¼ tsp black pepper
> 4 tbsp flour
> 3 tbsp butter
> 2 tbsp chopped onion
> 3 tbsp tomato puree
> ¼ cup bouillon
> ¼ cup red wine
> 1 cup sour cream

Mix the salt, pepper, and flour, pounding them thoroughly into the pieces of meat. Brown the steak on both sides in butter. Add the other ingredients except for the sour cream. Cover and simmer until the meat is fork-tender. Add the sour cream and simmer just to heat.

DAUBE OF BEEF PROVENÇALE   *Chianti*

Just as *"Périgordine"* always means truffles, so *"Provençale"* always foretells garlic. Garlic is a strange vegetable, misunderstood by most Americans, who think that the smallest possible amount is barely acceptable but larger quantities are ruinous. On the contrary, as an example, garlic soup, made entirely of garlic cloves in milk, does not taste noticeably of garlic nor does it "come back on you" tomorrow. With that preliminary reassurance, here is a *Provençale* recipe.

> 4 lb trimmed beef brisket in 2-inch cubes
> 4 large onions, quartered
> 2 whole heads of garlic (20 or more cloves, not mashed)
>   Peel of 1 orange, grated
> 1 tsp bay leaf extract
> 1 tsp thyme
>   Red wine to barely cover

One day in advance of use, in a heavy iron dutch oven, brown the meat chunks nicely on all sides in a mixture of half olive oil and half cooking oil. Sprinkle with salt and pepper. Add the peeled garlic cloves and other ingredients. Cover closely and simmer over low heat for 3 hours or until the meat is tender. Cool, refrigerate, and skim off the congealed fat. Heat to boiling the next day, just before serving with French or Italian hard rolls.

NEW MEXICAN
STACK ENCHILADAS   *Red Grape Wine*

There are essentially three methods of making enchiladas, depending somewhat on the region of origin and complexity of preparation. The Spanish-American type consists of rolled filled tortillas packed into a pan and baked bathed in a hot sauce. The Mexican style uses rolled filled tortillas also but bakes them individually just enough to melt the cheese but leave the onions near-raw. The American-Mexican style developed in the cowboy country of the Southwest. In this method of cooking, flat tortillas with layers of filling between are baked in stacks.

First, make the sauce as follows. Frizzle half a pound of ground beef in butter, cover with wine, and simmer until the wine is almost all evaporated. Add two cans of prepared enchilada sauce. If desired, substitute chopped leftover chicken or turkey meat for the beef.

Now, planning on four tortillas per stack, one stack per person, fry the tortillas quickly in oil until they soften. Build the stacks on sheets of foil or on oven plates. To make each stack, dip a tortilla in the sauce and lay it on the plate. Cover the tortilla with chopped onion, grated cheddar cheese, and a generous drizzle of sauce. Build the additional layers in the same way. After the last cheese and onion are added on top, make a central nest and into this break an egg. Put the stacks into a 350-degree oven until the cheese melts, the sauce is bubbly, and the eggs are cooked. (If preferred, the eggs can be fried sunny side up.) This takes about 20 minutes. Serve on the oven plates or slide the foil onto a heated plate. Do not try to transfer a stack from the foil to a plate or there will be a culinary disaster.

NEW ENGLAND POT ROAST   *Red Grape Wine*

This is not to be confused with the New England boiled dinner! In fact, nothing but nothing should *ever* be confused with the stark, watery boiled dinner.

> 4 lb bottom round pot roast of beef
> 3 tbsp flour
> 2 tsp salt
> ½ tsp black pepper
> 3 tbsp cooking oil
> ½ cup horseradish, grated, or 1 4-oz jar
> 1 cup whole cranberry sauce
> 1 tsp cinnamon
> 4 cloves
> 1 cup beef bouillon
> 2 cups red wine
> 16 small white onions
> 2 cups diced carrots

Dredge the meat in the flour mixed with the salt and pepper. Brown the meat on all sides in the oil in a heavy iron casserole. Mix the horseradish, cranberry sauce, cinnamon, cloves, bouillon, and wine and pour it over the meat. Bring to a boil and simmer for about 2 hours or until the meat is tender. Separately sauté the onions till brown, add the carrots, and cook

New England Pot Roast contains some surprise seasonings which raise the dish beyond the ho-hum level.

Our New England Braised Dinner has the distinction of being cooked in wine and bouillon instead of the usual uninteresting water.

about 2 minutes longer. Add to the casserole and cook covered for another 25 minutes or until everything is tender and done.

NEW ENGLAND BRAISED DINNER   *Rose Hip Wine*

Thousands may disagree, but for us, the two dishes which vie for bottom billing in our list of edibles are Irish stew and the New England boiled dinner. Simply boiling stuff in water is so unimaginative and dull! Water is excellent for laundry and bathing purposes but we cook with bouillon from our own stock pot or wines from our own bottles. A little water goes a long way with us, in cooking. Actually, our chicken bouillon is aspic; it gels firmly and we cook vegetables in it.

For our New England Braised Dinner, which should preserve the delicate flavors of the vegetables, we chose rose hip wine not only because it reminded us of the wild-rose brakes of that area but because it is a delicately flavored wine which is not obtrusive. For us, the combination is felicitous and delicious.

Use a piece of corned beef, allowing about half a pound per person, and soak the meat overnight in water to reduce the saltiness. In a casserole, brown the beef on both sides in cooking oil at medium-high heat. Then add a cup of bouillon and a cup of rose hip wine. Cover the casserole and braise in a 300-degree oven for 1½-2 hours. Add small carrots, parsnips, onions, potatoes, and wedges of cabbage, adding more liquid if needed. Continue to braise until the vegetables are tender but do not overcook. Salt to taste but use discretion, since the meat was salty. Slice the beef, arrange on a warmed platter surrounded by the vegetables, and spoon over all the casserole juices which you have reduced to half-volume by boiling over high heat. If there are leftovers, the meat and juices can be added to bouillon and water with a little sherry, as the base for an excellent borscht-type hearty soup.

~~~~~~

CHAPTER 5

Pork And Ham

Despite the fact that some ethnic groups do not eat pork, the pig is quite ubiquitous and is widely used for food throughout Europe, the Americas, all Asiatic countries, and even the Pacific islands. No enterprising Polynesian ever started out in his canoe on a voyage of exploration without a trussed pair of pigs, waiting to start a new colony on a distant island or atoll. Traditionally cooked very well done because of the former danger of porcine trichina parasites, pork is still cooked well done because it tastes better that way. It lends itself to a wide variety of delicious preparations. Pork seems to have a natural affinity for cooking with all of the fruit wines.

CROWN ROAST OF PORK   *Peach Wine*

For this impressive and magnificent dish, have your butcher use a whole loin of pork, sawing the vertebrae as usual and

One of our most dramatic presentations is Crown Roast of Pork. Here we have impaled a preserved kumquat on each rib end. The central space is filled with a forcemeat made from the between-the-rib chunks of trimmed meat.

removing the segments of meat between the ribs down to the loin. Then bend the loin into a circle with the rib ends pointing out and tie the roast in this position with heavy string. Cover the rib ends to prevent charring. Finely grind the segments of meat removed from between the ribs, add salt and pepper, and work in as much dry peach wine as the meat will take. Pack this filling into the cavity at the top of the crown roast. Rub the entire roast with salt and pepper, put it into an open roasting pan, and plan on baking about 45 minutes per pound in a 325-degree oven. When the meat has become heated through, usually in about an hour, pour at least 2 cups of dry peach wine over the roast and continue cooking. Add more wine from time to time and baste with wine to give a beautiful, tasty, brown crust with plenty of delicious pan juices. Before serving, remove the foil from the rib ends and on each rib impale a preserved kumquat; or use the paper frills furnished by the butcher. Serve the roast with spiced peaches and roasted potatoes. Serve the pan juices separately, thickened somewhat with flour if desired.

BRAISED HAM SLICES *Apple Wine*

Ham certainly is typically American although not an American native. The apple on the other hand, is a New World product and we think apple wine is especially good with ham.

Do buy the best-looking ½-inch-thick slices of ham you can find or, better still, slice them from a half-ham yourself. Put 2 such slices in a baking dish and heat in a 350-degree oven until the ham is hot through, about 15 minutes. Add enough apple wine to come almost to the top of the slices. Continue to cook at 350 degrees for another half-hour or more, basting several times. Served with apple sauce, this makes a great dinner or a Sunday brunch. Of course you realize that we are talking about one of the succulent cooked hams and not the miserable, dried-out, rock-hard poor things that some people cherish.

This huge slice of ham braised in apple wine is surrounded by cinnamon-apple slices which almost escape the platter.

Pieces of pork which we call medallions or cutlets are braised in sherry and smothered with mushrooms.

PORK CUTLETS
OR MEDALLIONS   *Sherry Amoroso*

We often buy fresh ham, shoulder roasts, and such lesser cuts for the purpose of cutting them up to make special dishes. We usually can get some fairly large pieces which we call cutlets, some nice but round smaller pieces which we call medallions, and scrappy material which we grind to make meat loaf mix or sausage. The small pieces of pork have to cook longer than similar pieces of veal or beef; so the pork recipes are not for use in the chafing dish.

Salt, pepper, and flour small pieces of thin-sliced pork and brown on both sides in butter. When ready to brown the second side, add sliced mushrooms, continuing to cook until meat and mushrooms are well done. Barely cover the meat with sherry and simmer until the meat is fork-tender. Dissolve a tablespoon of cornstarch in sherry and add it, stirring briskly. Cook until the sauce is clear. Serve the sauce separately over rice or on toast points.

DOUBLE-THICK PORK CHOPS   *Peach Wine*

Dredge double-thick, 1½-inch-thick pork chops in flour with salt and pepper added. Brown nicely on both sides in butter. Add peach wine, about ½ cup per chop. Cook uncovered in a casserole in a 350-degree oven for about an hour or until the juices run clear after fork prick. Serve garnished with peach halves or spiced peaches.

Double-thick Pork Chops are excellent prepared by the shake-and-bake procedure, but here they have been braised in wine in the oven.

BAKED HAM EN CROÛTE   *Red Grape Wine*

We use a boned, canned "square" ham because it makes a better appearance and the crust conforms to its straight lines more readily. We use ordinary piecrust mix but substitute red wine for the prescribed water. Roll the pie dough into sheets and cover the ham completely, moistening the seams with wine and pinching together firmly. From the scraps of pie dough, make various leaf and flower shapes or use a small cooky cutter to make decorations for the top of the croûte. Bake for only about an hour in a 350-

Ham en Croûte is surrounded by its decorated flaky crust. Usually, the meat shrinks away from the crust in cooking, posing a carving problem, but this ham cooperated fully.

degree oven because all that is needed is to heat the already cooked ham through and bake the crust. If the crust begins to get too brown, reduce the heat to 325 degrees. The problem in slicing this attractive presentation is that the meat always shrinks, leaving some space between it and the crust. This lets the crust break easily during attempts to slice and serve. An electric knife or serrated blade makes it possible to "saw" the ham without too much pressure, thus sparing the crust.

COUNTRY-STYLE PORK SPARERIBS
AND WINE BARBECUE SAUCE   *Chianti*

We regard trying to eat ordinary spareribs as tantamount to being on a meatless diet. The minuscule fragments of fat and other anatomic structures are practically devoid of muscle tissue. But we are pleased to have been introduced to the cut of pork called country-style spareribs. These obviously are from the short-rib area with gorgeous chunks of muscle.

Place a large number of chunks (5 to 6 pounds) of this meat into a big iron skillet or casserole. Use a lot because the leftovers warm up beautifully. Spoon sauce over the meat very generously, using the Barbecue Sauce, the recipe for which is given in chapter 13.

Cook covered for about 4 hours, or start an hour earlier if the meat is frozen, adding more sauce if needed. Spoon off some of the fat, if there is too much to suit you. Serve with crusty hot rolls of the French or Italian type. After warming up several times, the meat falls off the bones, which can be removed to leave a great hot sandwich filling for hamburger rolls.

This mountain of meat shows the luscious chunks found in the cut called country-style spareribs, in contrast to the usual stark pile of bones.

STUFFED DOUBLE-THICK
PORK CHOPS
Tea or Angelica Wine

Have your butcher cut loin pork chops 2 inches thick and you will need 1 chop per person. With a sharp boning knife, make as large a pocket as possible in each chop by the method described in chapter 1. To make the stuffing for 4 chops, take

> **2 cups day-old bread cubes**
> **Wine**
> ½ **stick butter**
> 1 **onion, chopped**
> **Sage, thyme, and oregano**
> **Salt and pepper**

Stuffed Double-thick Pork Chops braised in wine and served with stuffed fluted mushroom caps sounds very fancy but really is easy to prepare and delicious to eat.

Melt the butter and sauté the onion until soft. Add the bread cubes and brown them nicely. Moisten with wine until the stuffing will hold together. Season to taste with the herbs, salt, and pepper. Fill the pocket in each chop with the stuffing and close with toothpicks, skewers, or needle and string. Brown the chops in butter on both sides, place in a covered pan with about half a cup of wine per chop, and cook, covered, for 1½ hours in a 325-degree oven. Serve with spiced peaches or cinnamon apple rings.

ROAST LOIN OF PORK
Pear or Apricot Wine

We prefer a 5- or 6-pound center cut or loin end pork roast, or even better, a half pork loin, because the leftovers are so delicious. Rub the roast with salt and pepper, put it in an open roasting pan, and plan on baking an hour per pound in a 325-degree oven. When the meat has become heated through, usually in about half an hour, pour at least 2 cups of dry fruit wine over the meat. Renew the wine periodically, if needed, and baste to give a beautiful, tasty glaze with plenty of pan juices.

The serendipitous results are almost better than the roast alone. Leftovers are delicious on a cold meat plate or in pork-lettuce-tomato toasted sandwiches. Slices heated in some of the leftover gravy become a variety of open-face hot roast pork sandwich when served over biscuits. Leftover pork makes a tasty meat pot pie, and we always freeze some choice pieces to accumulate with leftover chicken or duck, lamb, and sausage for our favorite dish, Cassoulet (see chapter 7).

The most unusual bonus from roast pork is Pork Indonesia with its blend of exotic flavors. To make this, sauté ½ cup of chopped onion in 2 tablespoons of oil and add ¾ cup of chicken bouillon. Then stir in ¼ teaspoon of ground cardamom, ¼ teaspoon coriander, ¼ cup lemon juice, ¼ cup soy sauce, ¼ cup packed brown sugar, and ½ cup peanut butter. Add cayenne until a distinctly hot taste pleases your palate. This sauce may be served cold over pork slices, as the Indonesians do. Or the roast may be reheated in the oven, the hot slices

The fruit wines give Roast Loin of Pork a marvelous crusty brown glaze which is crunchy and not too greasy. The pan juices make an excellent sauce, plain or thickened.

placed on a bed of fluffy rice, and the heated sauce poured over it. The simplest method is to heat the slices of pork directly in the sauce and serve over rice. With this we serve peach or pear chutney.

PORK PARMIGIANA   *Chianti*

The parmigiana method is widely used for veal but we find it delicious for chicken, pork, liver, or even eggplant as a meat substitute. The general method is the same for all.

Use boneless pork slices, about ¼ inch thick. Dip them in beaten egg and Italian seasoned bread crumbs, and then brown the pieces nicely on both sides in half-and-half olive oil and cooking oil. Place the browned meat in individual au gratin dishes or cook in a casserole. Bake in a 325-degree oven for 45 minutes. Then cover the meat with Italian tomato sauce thinned with about half chianti red wine. Cover all with slices of mozzarella cheese and then a generous sprinkling of grated parmesan cheese. Leave in the oven until the mozzarella is melted, usually about 15 minutes, and the sauce is bubbly.

HAM LOAF
WITH WINE GLAZE   *Riesling, Cabernet, or Rose*

Modern hams are soft, succulent, lightly salted, and only moderately smoked—a far cry from the briny, bone-hard pride of Smithfield. Even so, ham is so distinctly flavored that it tends to overpower other ingredients in a combination dish. We get around this by "diluting" the ham and using wine.

> 1 lb ground ham
> 1 lb lean ground pork
> 3 eggs
> 1 cup of the chosen wine
> 1½ cups fine-crushed cereal, such as Wheaties
> 1 tbsp parsley
> 1 medium onion, ground

Ham loaf attains a beautiful glaze with a sweet wine-fruit sauce, served hot with the loaf after baking.

Mix all ingredients thoroughly. Decorate the bottom of a loaf pan with pineapple slices and pieces in any design that appeals to you. Pack the meat mixture into the pan without disturbing the pineapple. Bake for 2 hours at 350 degrees, basting the top of the loaf several times with the following sauce:

> 1½ **cups brown sugar**
> ¼ **cup pineapple juice**
> ¾ **cup wine**
> 3 **tsp hot prepared mustard**
> ½ **tsp fresh ground ginger**

Unmold carefully and marvel at your handiwork.

PORK SAUSAGE   *Plum Wine*

Sausage, originally made as a method of preservation in the prerefrigeration days, is quite versatile, being used for breakfast or brunch, as a stuffing for roulades of beef, in the various dressings and stuffings for fowl, and as the main meat with sauerkraut. Unless you have a very favorite boughten sausage, it is easy and fun to make your own.

        4½ lb ground pork, 1 part fat to 2 parts lean
        4 tsp salt
        1 tsp black pepper
        1 tsp bay leaf extract
        1 tsp ground allspice
        ½ tsp cayenne
        ½ tsp thyme
        ½ tsp paprika
        ½ tsp garlic
        ½ cup plum wine

Grind the meat twice or 3 times to make it cohere better. Then thoroughly mix all the ingredients. Fry a small patty to test the seasoning and adjust as needed. We put up the sausage in ordinary freezer containers. We make some into patties separated by waxed paper, freezing them stacked; the remainder is made into rolls, rolled in cheesecloth, and twisted at intervals to form links. This sausage can be used to make Beef Roulades or, when shaped into balls, Breast of Chicken en Brochette.

SAUSAGE ROLLS AND SAUERKRAUT   *Plum Wine*

Sauerkraut with knockwurst is the traditional dish but unless you can get imported knockwurst, forget it! A knockwurst is just an overgrown hot dog and after learning of the weird and offensive trash included in American knockwurst, we became completely disenchanted. A good substitute is rolls of homemade sausage. We have never bothered with sausage casings, which one can buy, but are happy with the roll-in-cheesecloth method we have described in the preceding recipe.

Soak a pound of sauerkraut for an hour or so in cold water, rinse several times, and drain well in a sieve. Place the sauerkraut in a casserole with 1 apple, peeled and sliced, and 1 medium onion, sliced. Add 3 or 4 crushed juniper berries and sauté all this in butter until the apple and onion are done. Add bouillon and plum wine half and half to barely cover the sauerkraut. Lay on enough sausage rolls, with cheesecloth removed, to cover the top of the sauerkraut. Cover the casserole and bake for 2 hours at 325 degrees.

CHAPTER 6

~~~~~~

Veal

In some countries where beef is not a prominent meat, veal is plentiful and popular. This apparently is true in Italy, for example, but how does one get a supply of little cows without having big cows? Veal must be cooked well done or else it has the same slick unpleasant feel as does underdone chicken. We must admit that veal is not our favorite meat, partly because it always is so scrappy, but nonetheless, some great things can be done with it. Here are some of the veal dishes we enjoy, and do not forget to refer back to chapter 2 for a great veal pâté.

VEAL MEDALLIONS   *Sherry Amoroso*

Medallions of veal or pork properly should be cut as very thin slices from the "eye" or from the tenderloin, but we use very thin slices from roasts, trimmed to about 2-3 inches in diameter, or thicker pieces pounded out. To us, medallions are thin rounded pieces somewhat like the pieces used for wienerschnitzel or veal parmigiana, only smaller. By partially cooking the meat in the kitchen, this dish becomes a spectacular chafing dish offering, to be finished at tableside with flair. It even lends itself to flaming with brandy if one wants to go all the way.

Allow about 4 medallions, up to 3 inches in diameter, per person. Dredge the meat in flour, salt, and pepper; then sauté the pieces in butter until nicely browned on both sides. Add about a half-cup of fresh sliced mushrooms per person and continue to sauté until the mushrooms have given up their moisture. Canned, drained mushrooms may be substituted, if desired. Half-cover the meat and mushrooms with sherry and continue to simmer until the meat is fork-tender. Add salt and pepper to taste, if needed. Usually, by this time the pan juices have reduced and thickened from the dredging flour, but if desired, thickening can be enhanced by adding a little flour dissolved in sherry. Stir in carefully and cook until the sauce is done. Serve on heated plates with a vegetable and a tossed salad.

Veal Medallions may be prepared in a chafing dish or more prosaically in a skillet. A pretty preparation and presentation adds much pleasure to the good taste.

OSSO BUCO

In our younger days, when we were ignorant but knew everything, the mere mention of "stew" was enough to set up uncontrollable gagging because to us the word meant an uninspired New England boiled dinner or that even more insipid Irish stew, both made with *water*, of all things. In more recent times, we have learned that most nations have some perfectly delectable stews, which do not deserve that maligned name. A good stew is made with bouillon or stock base, with lots of good wine, plus delightful meats, vegetables, and herbs. We have fantastic stew recipes from many nations and regret our years of darkness. One of the most outstanding of all stews is the osso buco of the Italians. Traditionally, osso buco, which means marrowbone, is made from veal shanks but we find beef shanks easier to obtain, more economical, much more meaty, more hearty in flavor, and highly delicious. We follow tradition only by describing it among the veal dishes.

1 2½-inch segment of veal or beef shank per person
2 cups onions, finely chopped
1 cup carrots, finely chopped
1 cup celery, finely chopped
1 tsp garlic, finely chopped
4 tbsp butter
Salt
Pepper
Flour for dredging meat
¼ cup olive oil
1 cup plum wine
½ tsp basil
½ tsp thyme
2 bay leaves crumbled, or 1 tsp bay leaf extract
Handful of parsley
¾ cup bouillon
1 pt canned tomatoes

Melt the butter in a heavy casserole and when it is through foaming, add the chopped vegetables, stirring often for about 15 minutes, until this mirepoix is soft and lightly colored. Remove from heat and reserve. Salt and pepper the meat, dredge it in

Osso Buco traditionally is a veal shank stew, but we substitute beef shank segments because of their greater meatiness, availability, flavor, and economy. Usually one segment of the size shown will serve two persons.

flour, and brown the pieces on all sides in the heated olive oil. Then stand the pieces of meat upright in the casserole, atop the vegetables. Deglaze the meat pan with the wine and then add the bouillon, tomatoes, and all the herbs, bringing this to a boil and then pouring it over the meat and vegetables. Adjust the liquid to come about halfway up the sides of the meat. Cover the casserole and bake for about 2½ hours in a 350-degree oven.

To serve, arrange the meat on a heated platter and spoon the vegetables and sauce around it. For an added visual and taste treat, sprinkle the meat with gremolata, made by mixing 1 teaspoon grated lemon peel, 1 teaspoon finely chopped garlic, and 3 tablespoons finely chopped parsley. Serve with pasta, rice, or Italian bread. This marvelous stew freezes so well that we usually make a double recipe to thaw and rewarm for later use. Most often, there is excess sauce and vegetables which we add to the perpetual soup pot. Oh, yes, do not forget to eat and enjoy the big chunks of marrow. You may need to use seafood forks to get it out. *Buono appetito!*

STUFFED ROLLED VEAL ROAST   *Chenin Blanc*

Veal is a "soft" meat whose connective tissues have not had time to develop; so roasts tend to fall apart. Also, a small carcass of veal gives small, thin pieces of meat. For these reasons, breast of veal, the heaviest part except for the thigh, usually is rolled and tied with string to maintain shape for cooking and slicing. So, either buy a breast of veal or a roast already rolled and tied. Either way, open out the slab of meat, trim it, and remove the white fibrous tissue. Salt and pepper the surfaces.

For the stuffing, cook a long-grain wild rice mix according to the directions on the package but substitute chenin blanc wine for the prescribed water. If desired, add some chopped onion. Let the stuffing cool and stir in a beaten egg. Spread the meat with this mixture, roll fairly snugly and tie in 3 or more places. This roll is a little difficult to handle but brown it in oil on all sides, turning as carefully as possible. Sprinkle the surface with paprika, purely for appearance, and bake covered 1 hour in a 350-degree oven. Then bake half an hour uncovered, basting frequently with chenin blanc. Thicken the pan juices with cornstarch in wine and consider adding some sliced mushrooms.

VEAL PARMIGIANA   *Chenin Blanc*

This recipe uses veal in the same type of slices as described for Pork Parmigiana and the recipe is identical, substituting chenin blanc for the chianti to give a lighter touch to the more delicate meat.

VEAL CUTLETS   *Rose Hip Wine*

We use veal steaks, which actually are the same as a T-bone cut of beef. These we pan-fry until nearly done and then half-cover with rose hip wine, simmering until the wine is reduced at least by half. Thicken the pan juices with cornstarch in a little wine. Cook until clear.

CHAPTER 7

Lamb

It probably is safe to say that of all the major meats used in the United States, lamb is the least popular. This undeserved position of low esteem may be because much of the imported lamb has a taste between that of a ram and a goat. In the Islamic countries, on the other hand, lamb is almost the only meat not frowned upon by religious beliefs. We seem to fall someplace in between these two extremes of opinion, finding lamb, both rare and well-done, a great delicacy, particularly when cooked with wines.

ROAST LEG OF LAMB   *Quince Wine*

One of the most ancient of fruits, quinces came originally from the Middle East, where some scholars have identified them as the probable apple of Eden. Not a favorite fruit in the United States

Roast Leg of Lamb, well done with quince wine, is an emir's dish. Note that the French method of carving is used, making horizontal slices which give more and better serving pieces.

and rather difficult to find, you should locate your quince supply before making any further plans. Formerly, we had a kind friend who supplied us with about half a bushel of quinces every fall, from which we made quince honey, jam, candy, chutney, liqueur, and wine. This source finally dried up but by that time we had a four-year supply of the wonderful wine. A few years ago, a generous lady advertised in the paper for people to come pick quinces from her two trees. We got there within the hour and came away with a bushel.

   We use half or preferably a whole leg of lamb because we want plenty of leftovers. The meat is rubbed with salt and pepper, placed in an open pan, and popped into a preheated 325-degree oven. When the meat is heated through, usually in about half an hour, pour at least 2 cups of quince wine over it and continue basting with more wine from time to time. Allow at least half an hour per pound for well-done lamb, which is the way we like it in this instance. The pan juices make a delicious thickened gravy.

LAMB SHANK STEWS FROM
AROUND THE WORLD

Various Wines

For each of the following ethnic recipes for lamb shank stew, plan on two segments of meat per person and for *each* of the following recipes, prepare the meat as follows:

Rub the meat with salt and pepper. Dredge in flour and brown nicely on all sides in half-and-half olive oil and cooking oil. Remove from heat and reserve.

ITALIAN

2 onions, chopped
½ green pepper, chopped
1 zucchini, sliced
1 cup tomatoes
  Cooking oil
  Olive oil
½ cup Italian sausage, removed from casing
1 cup rose wine
½ tsp oregano
½ tsp thyme
½ tsp basil
½ tsp salt
  Bouillon

Lamb shanks are quite meaty, as lamb cuts go, and they can be flavored in many ethnic ways. This is the Italian way.

Italian Lamb Shank Stew is a hearty meal, one lamb shank being an ample serving for most persons.

Sauté all the vegetables in half cooking oil half olive oil until soft and then add the crumbled sausage, continuing to frizzle. When the sausage is done, add the seasonings and wine. Simmer about 10 minutes. Arrange the meat in a casserole on top of the vegetables and adjust with bouillon and wine so that the meat is about half-covered. In a 350-degree oven, cook covered for about 1½ hours. Arrange the meat on a heated platter and spoon the vegetables and sauce over it.

FRENCH
2 cups onions, chopped
1 carrot, chopped
1 cup sliced fresh mushrooms
1 stalk celery, chopped
1 tsp tomato paste
1 cup vermouth
1 tsp dry tarragon
  Bouillon

Sauté the vegetables and proceed as in the Italian recipe.

AMERICAN

4 medium potatoes, quartered
2 onions, chopped
1 cup tomatoes
2 parsnips, sliced
1 bay leaf, crumbled, or 1 tsp bay leaf extract
1 cup dandelion wine
Bouillon

Boil the potatoes and parsnips in barely enough bouillon to cover, until just tender. Then add the onions, tomatoes, bay leaf, and wine. Simmer about 15 minutes. Put the meat atop the vegetables in a covered casserole and cook at 350 degrees for about 1½ hours. Serve as before.

NEAR EAST

1 small eggplant, diced
2 onions, chopped
Olive oil
1 cup tomatoes
½ cup cooked chick peas
1 cup yogurt
2 tbsp pine nuts
Pinch of saffron
1 cup quince wine
Bouillon

Sauté the eggplant and onions in olive oil until barely soft; then add the other ingredients, except saffron, and simmer for about 10 minutes. If too dry, add more wine and bouillon. Just before completion, add the saffron. Combine the meat and vegetables in a casserole and cook as before.

FAR EAST

2 cups onions, chopped
1 medium apple, peeled, cored, and diced
Butter
1 tbsp curry powder
½ cup Coconut Milk (see chapter 1)
1 cup riesling
Bouillon

Sauté the onions and apple in butter until soft and then add the curry powder. Stir in; then add the coconut milk and wine, substituting rice wine if you wish. Simmer 5 minutes. Arrange the meat in a casserole and pour the vegetable mixture over it. Add enough bouillon to half-cover the meat and cook as before.

POLISH
½ **head of cabbage in wedges**
1 **can tiny whole beets**
1 **can tiny whole potatoes**
½ **tsp caraway seeds**
½ **tsp crushed juniper berries**
6 **chunks Polish sausage**
1 **cup zinfandel**
Bouillon

Place the browned meat in a casserole and surround it with the vegetables and herbs. Add the wine and lay on the sausage. Pour in enough bouillon to half-cover the meat. Cover and cook at 325 degrees for 2 hours. Serve as before.

LAMB PATTIES   *Pear Wine*

Those not particularly fond of the distinctive flavor of lamb may be pleasantly surprised at the improvement made by using one of the fruit wines, such as pear, peach, or quince. For this, grind scrappy lamb meat, removing as much of the fat as possible to minimize the lamb taste. Into the ground meat, work as much of the chosen wine as it will take. Fry the patties, either rare or well-done, and if desired, add some wine to simmer with the patties for the last 5 minutes or so.

CASSOULET   *Dandelion or Tea Wine*

Cassoulet is a traditional provincial French white bean casserole with several kinds of meats. Controversy rages about which of several versions is truly authentic because in one region cassoulet is made to use up all the goose meat left over from making pâté de foie gras, while in another area, there is a lot of lamb available and in a third, pork seems to be the most plentiful. Actually, cassoulet contains lamb, pork, fowl (chicken, turkey, duck, or goose), sausage, and white beans, in various proportions. The typical French cassoulet starts from scratch in the winter, using all fresh, uncooked meats. Everything is cooked separately, then assembled and baked. The casserole then goes onto the back porch to freeze and to be kept going all winter by adding more ingredients as they are needed. We make cassoulet to use leftover meats. Whenever we have roast lamb, pork, or any fowl, we freeze choice large pieces, usually in their own juice, holding them until we have a large enough volume and a sufficient variety of meats. We have limited ourselves to pork, lamb, and fowl with sausage although there is no good reason, except tradition, for not using roast beef or other meats. Cassoulet warms up beautifully and gets better with each rewarming. We refrigerate the casserole, add to it, and usually keep it going for at least a month by heating it for dinner about once a week. Using leftover meats makes cassoulet a lot simpler than the complicated chore the French make of it. Here is how we do it.

> **1½ lb navy beans**
> **4 cups bouillon**
> **1 cup tea or dandelion wine**
> **1 tsp salt**
> **1 tsp bay leaf extract**
> **1 cup chopped onion**
> **1 cup bread crumbs**
> **2 tbsp dried parsley**
> **8 cooked sausage patties or slices of kielbasa Polish**
> **sausage**
> **Chunks of leftover meat of types mentioned**

Cover the beans with water and soak them overnight. Then cook the beans in the wine and bouillon with the bay leaf, onion, and salt until the beans are soft but not mushy. Adjust seasoning if needed. To assemble the cassoulet, put about a fourth of the cooked beans into a 4-quart casserole. Then place a layer of roast lamb meat and another layer of beans. Next,

Cassoulet is without a doubt the world's best baked bean dish. With its diversity of meats and its facility for tasting better with each rewarming, it is a great dish to keep around for weeks at a time.

make a layer of roast pork and a layer of beans. Finally, use the remaining meats except the sausage and cover with the remaining beans. Put the sausage in a layer on top of all. Add liquid left from cooking the beans, with enough more wine and bouillon to bring the liquid to the lowermost part of the top layer of beans. Cover the top with the bread crumbs mixed with the parsley. Bake in a 300-degree oven for 2½ -3 hours.

Some recipes call for pushing the top layer of crumbs down into the juices at least twice during cooking, putting on additional crumbs each time, but our casserole always is too full of beans and meat to permit this.

LAMB STEAKS   *Pear or Peach Wine*

Smaller pieces of lamb meat in the form of steaks, chops, cutlets, medallions, or whatever, are improved by wine. We fry the meat in butter until almost done and then add enough fruit wine to almost cover the meat. We let this simmer for 4-5 minutes. The pan juices are thickened with cornstarch in more wine. This gravy is especially good over fluffy rice.

Lamb Steaks are more palatable to more people if trimmed of all fat and braised in wine.

LAMB RAGOUT   *Red Grape Wine*

One immediate bonus from Roast Leg of Lamb with Quince Wine (see recipe earlier in this chapter) is Lamb Ragout served over biscuits, noodles, or rice. For this cut all the scrappy meat off the bone. Then in 2 tablespoons of oil, sauté a cup of chopped onions until transparent and add the lamb meat in chunks. Continue to sauté until the onions start to brown and then add a pint of canned or fresh tomatoes with three whole cloves. Simmer this for about an hour and shortly before serving, stir in the leftover lamb gravy. This is a dish fit for an Arabian prince and agreeable to most American palates.

CHAPTER 8

~~~~~~

Poultry

From such unlikely beginnings as jungle fowl of Southeast Asia, wild turkeys of the American forest, ducks from the ponds of China, and guineas from the jungle of Africa have come a huge variety of edible birds. When the many game birds and even song birds are considered, the poultry-fowl-bird group furnishes thousands of tantalizing recipes. Chicken alone is the delicious principal ingredient of many international dishes.

**CORNISH
GAME HENS**   *Dandelion or Tea Wine*

We buy the 1½ - to 2-pound cornish game hens by the dozen, storing them in the freezer. The hens can be thawed over a 2-day period in the refrigerator, overnight in the kitchen sink, or in a pan of water for 6 hours, depending on the speed needed. Remove the wrapped package of neck and giblets from the body cavity and wash each bird well. Then, salt and pepper inside and out. Put 2 birds in a 6-quart casserole, open, in a 450-degree oven for half an hour, till the skin begins to brown. Now, pour wine over the birds, using at least a cup of wine per bird. Continue baking at 325 degrees, uncovered, for another 2 hours. There is no need to baste the hens, but inspect them after an hour to see if more wine should be added. At serving time, the little hens are very juicy and tender with a beautifully glazed brown crackly skin. The pan juices are rich and dark brown, suitable for making gravy, for use "as is" over biscuits, or for reserving for one of the serendipitous uses.

Usually, we cannot eat a whole bird each; so we almost always salvage a moderate amount of meat. Part of this finds its way into toasted chicken-lettuce-tomato sandwiches for lunch or brunch. The remainder is refrigerated for later use. The greatest bonus from the little hens is the bouillon which we have mentioned in some detail.

Cornish Game Hens make a great dinner, allowing one bird per person, but few will fail to leave some highly useful leftovers for sandwiches, hot dishes, pâté, bouillon, and what not. Roasted with dandelion, tea, or plum wine, they are delicious.

Some days later the rest of the meat shows up in a delightful authentic curry. One medium-sized chopped onion and half of a sliced apple are sautéed in 2 tablespoons of butter until the onion is transparent and the apple slices are soft. Then add 1-2 teaspoons of curry powder and a half-cup of bouillon plus a cup of Coconut Milk (see directions for making in chapter 1). Simmer all this for a few minutes and add the chicken meat. Continue to cook until the meat is hot; then salt to taste and serve over fluffy rice with peach chutney and other curry accompaniments.

With a gourmet boost from the dandelion or tea wine, two little cornish game hens give us an entree of roast chicken, a sandwich for lunch, about a quart of all-purpose bouillon, and an entree of curried chicken plus liver pâté hors d'oeuvres or a brunch of sherried livers on toast. So much from so little but so delicious!

ROULADES OF
CHICKEN BREAST *Tomato Wine*

Always on the lookout for dry wines which will not be too sweet for cooking, light-colored wines which will not make a "muddy" appearance in an entree, and bland wines which will not be of too pronounced a flavor, we were pleased to discover all three attributes in tomato wine.

Chicken, the most versatile and widely used of all meats, is difficult to present in a new guise. We believe we have done it, however, in a distant but more sophisticated cousin of chicken Kiev. Without being either a butcher or a surgeon, you, too, can bone a whole chicken breast, ending up with all the meat in one piece, although somewhat precarious and tenuous in the midline. Just take a sharp little boning knife and push-cut all the meat from the breast bone and wishbone down to the rib beginnings. If the meat is too thick to roll well, either remove the "filet" piece or pound the meat to the desired thickness. To prepare the roulade, lay out one of the sheets of chicken breast meat, salt and pepper it lightly, and spread a fairly thick layer of Chicken Liver Pâté over all (see chapter 2 for pâté recipe). Over

Chicken Roulades, elegant cousins of chicken Kiev, are stuffed with our special Chicken Liver Pâté and braised in wine.

the pâté layer, sprinkle finely chopped onion followed by a generous layer of crumbled tarragon leaves. Then roll the meat rather tightly and tie securely in several places with string. Plan on one roulade per person and dredge the required number in flour. Brown them nicely on all sides in butter in a casserole. Add enough tomato wine to cover the roulades about halfway, or use about half a cup of wine per roulade. Cover the casserole and bake in a 325-degree oven for an hour. Thicken the pan juices with cornstarch in tomato wine or use a little cream if you prefer. Serve the sauce over the roulades or pass it separately. Leftovers can be frozen for later use, sliced thin in an excellent sandwich, or crumbled into a very elegant omelette.

WINE-INJECTED TURKEY BREAST   *Plum Wine*

A 6- to 8-pound turkey breast with the skin left on is just right, quite festive, and furnishes plenty of leftover meat for many gourmet uses. Using a baster-injector with needle attached, inject about a cup of dry plum wine, distributing it fairly evenly under the skin of the whole breast. With a small-caliber needle, little if any wine leaks out through the needle puncture holes. Rub the breast with softened butter and then bake it in a 325-degree oven with about 2 cups of the wine in the pan, baking about half an hour per pound or until the skin is a rich golden brown and the juices run clear after pricking the skin with a fork. No basting is necessary. Let the breast rest about 15 minutes before slicing the succulent meat. The abundant pan juices make a delicious thickened sauce if desired.

Serendipitous dishes from leftovers are many with roast turkey breast. The traditional club sandwich of turkey, bacon or ham, cheese, tomato, and lettuce can be varied in the Scandinavian manner by making an open-faced work of art. Heated in gravy, a deliciously flavored hot turkey sandwich results, or the meat and gravy can be served over biscuits or rice.

Turkey pâté is an excellent cocktail-time addition, made from 2 cups of ground turkey meat with 1 small onion. Add 2 tablespoons brandy and enough softened butter to make a very smooth pâté which holds its shape. Add ⅛ teaspoon allspice, a

Turkey breast injected with plum wine develops a marvelous crusty brown skin with moist succulent meat beneath it.

dash of nutmeg, and a dash of cloves. Salt and pepper to taste. For a zestier pâté, add cayenne to suit your palate.

An excellent use for leftover turkey meat is in turkey Tetrazzini. This uses 2-3 cups of the shredded meat. To about 2 cups of the gravy, add 2 tablespoons plum wine, ½ cup blanched slivered almonds, and 1 cup sautéed mushrooms. Place the meat in individual au gratin dishes, cover with the sauce, sprinkle with grated parmesan cheese, and bake at 375 degrees until bubbly and lightly browned.

Another leftover dish with an Italian twist is turkey parmigiana. Arrange slices of turkey meat in individual au gratin dishes and sprinkle with plum wine to moisten. To Italian-seasoned tomato sauce, add chopped mushrooms and finely chopped onion. Cover the meat slices with sauce, sprinkle on a thin layer of grated parmesan cheese, and lay slices of mozzarella cheese over all to cover. Bake at 375 degrees until bubbly and lightly browned.

BRAISED
CHICKEN HALVES   *Mulberry-Ginger Wine*

We have dozens of great chicken recipes and always are originating or discovering new approaches. We gave up on fried

Mulberry-ginger wine comes into its own when used to braise chicken halves.

chicken years ago as being quite unrewarding, but we do not have time enough to try all of the other great ways to prepare chicken. We buy chickens in all degrees of dismemberment, any of which are acceptable, but we mention whole chicken breasts of chicken halves so there will be plenty of leftovers.

Brown 1 whole chicken breast or chicken half per person in half butter, half oil. When brown on all sides, add at least a half-cup of mulberry-ginger wine for each piece of chicken and braise in the oven until thoroughly cooked (about 1½ hours). Add more wine if necessary. Make the usual uses of the excellent pan juices.

CINNAMON CHICKEN HALVES   *Sherry Amoroso*

We figured this recipe out, following a delightful luncheon with Chinese friends at one of the country clubs in New Territory near Hong Kong.

The cinnamon-soy-honey-sherry marinade for Cinnamon Chicken Halves is very ropy from the cinnamon and must be poured on or, better, painted on with a brush. The end result is delectable.

Cinnamon Chicken Halves is a typical Chinese dish which we encountered in New Territory outside Hong Kong.

1 chicken half per person
¼ cup honey
½ cup sherry
¼ cup soy sauce
2 tbsp powdered cinnamon

Mix the sauce thoroughly and marinate the chicken halves in it for at least an hour at room temperature. This sauce is very thick and has a very strange ropy consistency from the cinnamon. We apply the marinade with a small brush and baste several times. After marinating, re-cover the pieces of chicken with the sauce and bake in an open pan at 325 degrees for 1½ hours, basting frequently. The chicken will be almost black, with a wonderful glazed crust.

CHICKEN MOLE POBLANO   *Red Grape Wine*

People usually think of chocolate only in the connotation of a sweet drink or dessert, but the Mexicans know that bitter chocolate combines in exotic ways with meats. This recipe uses chocolate with chicken. To make the mole poblano sauce you need

2 green peppers
¼ tsp anise seed
4 tbsp sesame seeds
1 clove garlic
¾ cup almonds, blanched and toasted
3 tbsp chili powder
½ tsp cinnamon
¼ tsp clove
½ tsp coriander
½ tsp cumin
1½ tsp salt
¼ tsp red pepper
1 cup onion
1 square bitter chocolate
1 1-lb can tomatoes
3 tbsp cooking oil
½ cup red wine
Bread crumbs

Put all the ingredients except bread crumbs in the blender and whirl at high speed until fairly smooth. Then gradually add bread crumbs until the sauce is quite thick and almost a paste. The sauce freezes well and when thawed, it may be thinned with a little wine and bouillon.

We use chicken thighs or half-breasts. Put the pieces in a casserole and spread each piece generously with mole poblano sauce. Bake covered at 325 degrees for 1½ hours. Add more sauce from time to time if needed.

Many meat dishes based on chocolate are originally Mexican; Chicken Mole Poblano is a very worthy example.

Chicken Paprikash is one of the sour cream dishes of which the Central European countries can be proud. It is distinctive.

CHICKEN PAPRIKASH   *Chenin Blanc*

The sour cream dishes most often involve veal or some of the beef cuts, but there is no reason why chicken should be ignored.

> **Chicken breasts or thighs**
> **Salt and pepper**
> **2 tbsp cooking oil**
> **1 cup onions, chopped**
> **½ tsp chopped garlic**
> **1½ tbsp sweet paprika**
> **½ cup chicken bouillon**
> **½ cup chenin blanc**
> **2 tbsp flour**
> **1½ cups sour cream**

Salt and pepper the chicken pieces and nicely brown them on all sides in hot oil. Remove and reserve the chicken. Sauté the onions and garlic in the oil until lightly colored. Off heat, stir in the paprika. On heat, add the bouillon and wine and bring to a boil to deglaze the pan. Return the chicken to the pan and simmer about half an hour or until the juices run clear yellow. Mix the flour and sour cream. Stir in carefully and simmer 6-10 minutes until the sauce is thick, smooth, and without raw flour taste. Serve with spaetzle.

CHICKEN
GROUND NUT STEW   *Rose Hip Wine*

In countries where cooking is done over an open fire or brazier with few utensils, the national cuisine runs heavily to stews, which can be excellent and exotic. A typical African stew is as follows:

> **Chicken thighs, 2 per person**
> **Cooking oil**
> **2 large onions, sliced**
> **1 pt tomatoes**
> **1 cup rose hip wine**
> **½ cup Coconut Milk (see chapter 1 for recipe)**
> **¼ cup chunky peanut butter**
> **Salt and pepper to taste**
> **Dried cayenne to taste**

Brown the chicken pieces in oil and add the onion slices. Cook until the onions are transparent and lightly brown. Add all the

Chicken with an African twist is exemplified by Chicken Ground Nut Stew, ground nuts being peanuts, in case you did not know!

other ingredients and simmer 1½ hours or until the chicken is well done. This dish should be quite pepper-hot to be authentic. Serve with fluffy rice.

Chinese Almond Chicken is a fine example of the quick-cooking dishes which can be prepared on a brazier.

CHINESE
ALMOND CHICKEN   *Sherry Amoroso*

In many of the Chinese dishes the bite-sized pieces of meat are marinated in a mixture of soy sauce, sherry, cornstarch, and other ingredients. This system works well even when leftover cooked meat is being used.

> **1 cup cubes raw chicken meat**
> **1 cup almonds, blanched and toasted**
> **7 tbsp cooking oil**
> **½ cup mushrooms**
> **½ cup cubed, canned bamboo shoots**
> **½ cup cubes celery**
> **¼ cup chopped onions**
> **10 water chestnuts, peeled and cubed**
> **½ cup sherry**

Marinate the chicken for about an hour at room temperature in a mixture of 1 tablespoon cornstarch, ¾ teaspoon salt, 3 tablespoons soy sauce, 3 tablespoons sherry, 1 tablespoon grated fresh ginger, and 1 tablespoon mashed garlic. Spoon the liquid over the meat at intervals. Sauté the vegetables 1 minute in 3 tablespoons oil. Remove and reserve. Sauté the chicken cubes in 4 tablespoons oil for 2 minutes. Combine all the ingredients except the almonds and cook about 2 minutes. Serve on a heated platter with the almonds scattered on the top. Serve with fluffy rice.

COQ AU VIN   *Zinfandel*

This is a justly famous dish, an almost universal offering of French restaurants, and one of the few examples of chicken or any other white meat prepared with a red wine.

Use whatever chicken parts appeal to you and dredge them in flour. Brown them nicely on all sides in oil in a casserole. About

In almost all cases, chicken is cooked with white wine; but Coq au Vin is a great exception, being a chicken stew with red wine.

half-cover the chicken with half red wine and half bouillon. Simmer for an hour and then add small canned potatoes and small canned white onions. Continue to cook for another half-hour. The juices will thicken somewhat from the dredging flour but if a thicker sauce is wanted, stir in more flour in wine and cook a few minutes longer. Serve with hot French or Italian hard rolls.

TURKEY CHOW MEIN   *Sherry Amoroso*

An excellent chow mein is made from cubes of cooked turkey meat, marinated for several hours in ⅔ cup sherry, ⅓ cup soy sauce, 1 tbsp cornstarch, and ½ tsp chopped fresh ginger. Slice ½ cup onion and ½ cup celery, blanching a few seconds in boiling water and cooling immediately under cold water. In oil over high heat, sauté the onion and celery, adding ½ cup snow peas (with pods), ½ cup mushrooms, 1 cup bean sprouts, ½ can sliced bamboo shoots, and ½ can sliced water chestnuts. Remove the vegetables and sauté the meat just to heat through.

One of our favorite dishes using leftover turkey meat is Turkey Chow Mein, made with delightful stir-fried Chinese vegetables.

Add the vegetables and the marinade, cooking together until heated through. Adjust the seasoning or put soy sauce on the table. Serve over a bed of crisp Chinese noodles and sprinkle slivered blanched toasted almonds on top.

Another serendipitous by-product of leftover turkey is Turkey Pot Pie, a strictly American product.

TURKEY POT PIE   *Dandelion or Tea Wine*

A favorite way to use leftover turkey meat is in a delicious pot pie. We gauge the quantity of ingredients by the amount of meat and the number of pies to be made. We make the pot pies in individual baking dishes in which they freeze very well, especially before the crust is baked.

   1 cup cubed leftover turkey meat
   1 sliced onion
   2 cubed potatoes
   2 diced carrots
   ½ cup mushrooms
   ½ cup frozen peas
      Bouillon and wine
      Either bay, tarragon, oregano, thyme,
         or curry powder

Cook all the vegetables until about half-done, with the chosen spice, in half wine, half bouillon to cover. Thicken the juices with a little flour in wine and add the turkey cubes. Fill individual ramekins or one large casserole. Top with your favorite pie dough, or follow one of these two alternative suggestions. Use popover mix, prepared according to the directions, and cover the pie ingredients with a generous layer. Or thaw the frozen unbaked patty shells, combine enough of them to roll out into a sheet, and cut to fit the ramekins or the casserole. With the piecrust or popover top, bake about 45 minutes in a 350-degree oven. With the puff paste patty shell dough, it is best to make the pieces of proper size, bake them entirely and separately so as to prevent soaking, and then put the tops on the pies when they have baked half an hour. Bake another 15 minutes or until heated through.

ROAST TURKEY WITH CORN BREAD STUFFING   *Pear Wine*

We rarely roast an entire turkey anymore, usually settling for the separate breast, but the entire bird calls for stuffing. We always detect an unpleasant taste and odor in turkeys stuffed before any cooking; so we invariably roast a 12-pound turkey about an hour at 325 degrees and *then* stuff it. The world's best stuffing, even when baked in a casserole to go with a turkey breast, is made as follows:

> 1 lb pork sausage
> 1½ cups chopped onion
> 1 cup chopped celery
> 5 cups crumbled corn bread
> 1 6-oz can mushrooms, chopped
> 1½ cups chopped pecans
> ¼ cup pear wine
> ¼ cup mushroom juice
> ¼ cup dried parsley
> ¼ tsp thyme
> ¼ tsp nutmeg

Frizzle the sausage and break it up so that there are no lumps.

We rarely roast a whole turkey anymore, but small birds give a lot of left-over meat with many possibilities plus a carcass for bouillon-making. Also, they provide a good excuse to make great stuffings, which we purposely make in large amounts for separate baking.

Add to the crumbled corn bread. Sauté the onion and celery in the sausage fat until soft and brown. Combine all the ingredients. Salt and pepper to taste. Stuff the turkey after it has baked an hour and, subtracting this from the total roasting time of about 20 minutes per pound, continue baking at 325 degrees. Excess dressing can be baked in a separate casserole. It freezes, thaws, and heats up beautifully.

ROAST LONG ISLAND DUCKLING
WITH RASPBERRY WINE SAUCE *Plum Wine*

Ducks and geese have such a thick layer of fat that they do not lend themselves well to marinating, nor can you very well cook them in wine unless you repeatedly draw off the excess melted fat in the pan. Fortunately, the meat is quite moist and we usually content ourselves with a wine sauce to be served with the duckling. Any one of a number of fruit wines can be used to make the wine sauce but here we have chosen raspberry as a good surrogate to represent the group.

The Long Island duckling runs about 5 to 6 pounds, which makes 2 good servings, usually with enough meat salvaged to make Cassoulet (see chapter 7). Rinse the duckling well, pat dry, and apply salt and pepper inside and out. Place in a pan on a rack to keep the bird up out of the fat. Bake at 375 degrees for 1½ -2 hours, depending on how well done you like the meat. During the baking, baste from time to time with plum wine at the same time that you remove excess fat. The wine accumulates beneath the layer of melted fat and forms a good pan juice later.

To make the sauce, rapidly boil 1 cup of dry raspberry wine, reducing to about ¾ cup. Add 1 tablespoon sugar, 1 tablespoon butter, and 2 tablespoons cornstarch in 2 tablespoons duck cooking juices (no fat). Heat, stirring constantly until thickened and clear.

CHICKEN PAN AMERICAN   *Pineapple Wine*

Chicken is very agreeable to many flavor nuances and we have enjoyed trying the recipes from all climes and lands. Here is one with a tropical twist.

> **1 chicken, quartered**
> **2 tbsp cooking oil**
> **½ onion, chopped**
> **¼ tsp minced garlic**
> **½ cup pineapple wine**
> **2 cups tomatoes**
> **½ tsp bay leaf extract**
> **1 tsp thyme**
> **½ tsp or more dried red pepper**
> **1 cup mashed ripe bananas**
> **3 firm bananas, cut into 1-inch chunks**
> **½ tsp salt**

Brown the chicken in oil; add the onion and garlic, sautéing about a minute. Add all ingredients except the banana chunks.

Bring to a boil and simmer until the chicken is tender. Remove the chicken pieces to a heated platter. Add the banana chunks and cook until heated through, stirring constantly. Spoon the sauce over the chicken and serve with rice.

CHICKEN WITH GREEN SAUCE   *Riesling*

Just before the first frost, we always gather several gallon baskets of tiny green tomatoes, usually of the Early Salad or Tiny Tim variety. We pickle them in various ways, and some we simply put into glass jars with heavy salt brine for use in making green sauce. To make the sauce, toast ¼ cup blanched almonds and ¼ cup pumpkin seeds in a 300-degree oven until lightly browned. In the blender at high speed, whirl 1 10-ounce can of the small brine tomatoes with their brine. These are labelled "Tomatillo" and are available in all stores stocking Mexican and Puerto Rican foods. Add ¼ cup of fresh coriander or 1 teaspoon ground dry coriander, 1 hot chili pepper, 1 medium onion, ¼ teaspoon cinnamon, and ¼ teaspoon sugar. Add the nuts and seeds a few at a time and continue to blend until fairly smooth. Dilute the sauce with ½ cup riesling and a half-cup of bouillon.

Brown chicken thighs or breasts in oil in a casserole and then cover them with sauce. Bake in a 350-degree oven, basting occasionally, for 1½ hours. The sauce freezes well.

STUFFINGS FOR FOWL

In making stuffings, it is possible to express a great deal of ingenuity and initiative. Recipes are difficult to give with precise quantities because the body cavities of the various fowls differ so widely. In general terms, the long-grain wild rice mix, substituting wine for the water, makes the quickest, easiest, and possibly the most exotic stuffing. In the other stuffings, bread crumbs or cubes, cracker crumbs, or crumbled corn bread are the basis, being soaked with bouillon, wine, or a combination.

Something bland such as plum wine is good and not too over-powering. A cornmeal mush base can be used but this, like yams, is too solid and heavy. Other bases that may be used are grits, semolina, pilaf, or buckwheat groats, although the latter has a very decided flavor of its own.

The traditional seasoning is sage, but there is no reason why this must be so. Varying the seasoning with Italian, Near Eastern, Far Eastern, Northern European, or any other regional ingredients is worth trying (see Lamb Shank Stews in chapter 7 for some ideas). Various nuts are commonly used in stuffing, including pecans, walnuts, hazelnuts, peanuts, chestnuts, pine nuts, or pistachios.

Oysters traditionally have been added to a bread stuffing at holiday seasons. Some of the dried fruits give nice variety, being cooked first in wine. These include prunes, apricots, peaches, and apples, primarily. Be venturesome with stuffings. It breaks monotony!

CHAPTER 9

~~~~~~

Seafood

Fish respond best to poaching and broiling, being especially good with vermouth. Other denizens of the sea are somewhat more versatile and find their way into some highly delectable dishes which can be quite haute cuisine.

ROULADES OF SOLE   *White Grape Wine*

There is nothing original about rolling up a piece of meat and stuffing it with something. All nationalities do this but to use fish is a little unusual and our "invention" of roulades of sole stuffed with shrimp pâté and poached in white wine deserves a try.

First, make Shrimp Pâté, the recipe for which is given in chapter 2. Allow one filet of sole per person, spreading each filet with a thick layer of the shrimp pâté. Then sprinkle

Roulades of Sole braised in vermouth with tarragon make a delicious entree. The shrimp pâté stuffing is a great addition and taste treat.

generously with dried tarragon. Roll the filets tightly and tie securely with string in several places. Put the roulades into a baking dish and add enough white wine to come halfway up the roulades. Bake about 45 minutes in a 350-degree oven, uncovered, basting occasionally. Add more wine if needed. The liquid can be thickened with cornstarch and served as a sauce over the rolls. Any leftover juice can be added to the freezer container of court bouillon. There will not be any leftover roulades, we guarantee.

BAKED WHOLE RED SNAPPER   *Vermouth*

Although fish filets or chunks can be poached with vermouth, there is something more elegant about baking and serving a whole fish. We like a 5- or 6-pound fish, or whatever type is locally available, with the head left on but with tail and fins removed to prevent burning and unsightliness. Baked in vermouth, displayed on a large platter, surrounded by piped mashed potatoes and garnished with lemon slices, a real banquet dish is produced.

The fish should be scaled and cleaned, the mouth propped open, and the eyes removed along with the tail and fins but the head left on. Rub the fish inside and out with salt and pepper. Place it in a large oven pan and then fill the body cavity with a mirepoix of chopped celery, carrots, and onions. This is purely

Baked Whole Red Snapper is prepared by removing tail and fins but leaving the head in place.

for flavor and is not served with the fish. If the fish is of a type which flakes too easily on cooking, a layer of cheesecloth draped over it will help prevent it from falling apart. For fish chunks, some chefs wrap the pieces of fish in cheesecloth for easier removal from the pan but it is not always easy to remove the cloth! Depending on the size of the fish, pour 2 or more cups of vermouth over it and bake uncovered in a 350-degree oven for about 15 minutes per pound or until the meat is translucent and tends to flake easily with a fork. At serving time, remove

The Baked Whole Red Snapper is decorated with a piping of mashed potatoes, a row of lemon slices, and an olive for an eye. Here, the fish is displayed on a Hawaiian pig board of native wood.

the cheesecloth, if it has been used, scoop out the mirepoix, and lift the fish onto a heated platter with two wide spatulas. Pipe mashed potatoes around it or use a ring of rice or cooked vegetables. Place an olive to substitute for the eye. Sometimes a small orange or tomato looks good in the open mouth. Garnish with parsley and some slices of lemon and pimento. This dish is excellent served as a cold buffet, also.

Be sure to save the carcass, skin, scraps, the removed tail and fins, the head, and the mirepoix, boiling to make a court bouillon for freezing.

Any large fish of the region is suitable but try to get one with white, dry meat and not of the fatty type which is apt to have a stronger taste. For example, bluefish is highly prized along the East Coast but it has several strikes against it. First, its meat is a bluish slate gray which does not make a nice appearance. Second, its meat is very "wet" and does not flake nicely but seems soggy. Finally, the very fatty meat does have a strong flavor which some find objectionable. We would not want to disparage bluefish unduly and we do bake them, but you should know what you are getting into.

SHRIMP TARRAGON   *Vermouth*

Our first real experience with tarragon was on a visit to the island of Majorca, where we identified its delights for the first time. With many interesting uses, it is at the top of our list of favorite herbs and it is at its best in Shrimp Tarragon, a light entree which is great for a Sunday night supper. It does well as a chafing dish specialty.

> 36 medium or 18 jumbo shrimp
> 2 tbsp minced shallots
> Salt and pepper
> 1 tsp lemon juice
> 4 tbsp butter
> 3 tbsp cognac
> ½ tsp crumbled tarragon leaves
> ¾ cup sweet cream
> Flour to thicken
> Vermouth

Shrimp Tarragon usually is made with large shrimp marinated in wine, but medium or small shrimp will do just as well, although with less flair.

Melt the butter in a skillet or chafing dish and cook the shrimp until pink and firm. Salt and pepper lightly. Sprinkle in the shallots, tarragon, and lemon juice, and add the cognac. Ignite the cognac, spooning the sauce over the shrimp until the flame dies. Add the cream and the vermouth, simmering 5 minutes. Thicken the sauce as desired with flour and serve all on toast points.

Shrimp Tarragon, displayed here in a Chinese lobster dish, usually is served over toast points.

SHRIMP STROGANOFF   *Riesling*

Dishes which cook quickly and at relatively low heat make excellent chafing dish specialties. The sour cream Shrimp Stroganoff is no exception. The dish is prepared in exactly the same manner as Beef Stroganoff (see chapter 4), substituting shrimp for beef and white wine for a red one. For added flair, you may want to sauté the shrimp in butter and then flame them with cognac before proceeding with the rest of the operation.

BRAISED SHAD ROE   *Tomato Wine*

Fish roe is widely regarded as a great delicacy, whether served as caviar or in the various dishes of cooked roe. We have found shad roe to be very synergistic with tomato wine, which is bland enough not to obtrude its flavor. Sherry is equally good, making a hearty breakfast, brunch, or an elegant dinner entree. While we are speaking of shad roe, the egg masses of almost any large fish will substitute admirably.

Shad roe braised in wine is an excellent breakfast or brunch dish, with crisp bacon and lemon slices.

Use a set (two lobes) per person for a dinner entree or one lobe for breakfast or lunch. Do not remove the membranes, else the roe will disintegrate into thousands of individual tiny eggs. The membranes disappear in cooking, anyway. Place the lobes of roe in a pan and half-cover with tomato wine. Poach them over moderate heat for about 15 minutes, basting occasionally, until the lobes are firm and done. It is best not to try to turn them over as they may break up. Transfer the roe lobes to an oven pan, reserving the poaching liquid, place a rasher of bacon on each lobe, and braise in a 350-degree oven until the bacon is done to your liking. During this time, make toast and thicken the poaching liquid with cornstarch to make a fairly heavy sauce which will not unduly soak the toast. Season to taste with salt and pepper. When the bacon is done, arrange the lobes of roe on a heated plate on toast points, spooning sauce over all.

VATAPA FISH STEW   *Chenin Blanc*

This South American dish with an African twist uses the same sauce as does Chicken Ground Nut Stew (see chapter 8) but is distinctive and delicious. Since fish chunks tend to disintegrate into flakes if cooked too long or too vigorously, make the sauce first according to the ground nut stew recipe. Then add the fish chunks; we usually put in a quantity of medium shrimp also. Simmer until the shrimp are done and fish just begins to flake. We prefer a dry white fish meat such as sole, halibut, or fresh cod. Serve with biscuits, hard rolls, or corn bread.

CIOPPINO   *Chianti*

The French bouillabaisse is justly famous but all seaside countries have their own ways of seasoning the national fish stew. Since the fishermen of the West Coast, and especially the San Francisco area, are largely of Italian descent, it is only natural that their cioppino should feature red wine, olive oil, tomato sauce, and Italian seasonings.

We have a very deep and abiding aversion to fish stews in which all the inhabitants keep their clothes on! We do not appreciate the noisy, messy process of slurping sauce off assorted shells, carapaces, claws, and miscellaneous bones. Besides, it is very wasteful of good sauce, which we do not like filled with bits and pieces of shell and sand. So, as might be expected, we undress the sea denizens before consigning them to the pot. Obviously, fish stews were made originally of whatever appeared in the day's catch, and our stew contains whatever we can catch at the local fish market. Here are some suggestions for seafood that makes good cioppino: crabmeat from claws or in chunks; mussels and clams of whatever type; fish chunks of several types such as fresh cod, sole, halibut, or other filets; lobster tails; shrimps or prawns, or scallops.

First, make fish stock (court bouillon) in a large pot by boiling all the skin, bones, shells, carcasses, carapaces, and trimmings in about 6 cups of water or enough to cover. When the water comes to a boil, skim off the scum and add 1 large onion, coarsely chopped, 1 bay leaf, crumbled, 6 whole black peppercorns, and a teaspoon of salt. Simmer for about 20 minutes and then strain through a five sieve, pressing firmly.

To make the cioppino, you need:

4 cups fish stock
¼ cup olive oil
1 cup onion, chopped
1 tbsp garlic, chopped
1 can tomatoes
3 tbsp tomato paste
1 cup red wine
2 tbsp chopped parsley

Sauté the onion and garlic in the oil until translucent. Add the fish stock and the other ingredients, bringing to a boil and simmering for 15 minutes. Then add all the seafood pieces and simmer until the fish begins to flake. Serve in soup plates with plenty of hard rolls. To vary the flavor, try seasoning with tarragon, or for a Mediterranean twist, add a little saffron.

COQUILLES ST. JACQUES   *Vermouth*

This delicious and subtly delicate dish is identical with the recipe of the same name described in chapter 2. The only difference is that as an entree, it usually is baked in a large casserole although individual ramekins make an interesting presentation.

Coquilles St. Jacques as an entree is prepared in an oven dish. This hand-crafted Mexican-style dish lends some additional charm.

SHRIMP EN COQUILLE   *Vermouth*

This shrimp dish is made exactly like Coquilles St. Jacques (see chapter 2), substituting medium shrimp for the scallops. The flavor is different and very enjoyable.

POACHED AND BROILED
SHAD ROE   *Rose Hip Wine*

    1 set of shad roe (2 lobes) per person
    Lemon juice and butter
    Rashers of bacon
    Toast points
    Rose hip wine

As a dinner entree, pairs of lobes of shad roe are poached in wine and then broiled. The grapefruit shown here is a broiled half, served as a dessert (see Broiled Grapefruit).

Partially cover the sets of shad roe with wine and poach until the roe is set firm and has changed color. Brush with lemon juice and melted butter and place the sets with strips of bacon alongside on a preheated broiler. When the bacon is nearing the crisp stage, place it atop the sets of roe. When done, serve the roe and bacon on hot toast points. This is an excellent dinner entree or a great treat with Sunday brunch.

FRESH COD AND
SALMON CROQUETTES   *Riesling*

There should be a strict law against inflicting salt cod in any of its guises on a helpless public, but fresh cod is a delicious fish. In these days of refrigeration, what is the excuse for salting and then soaking for days in a vain endeavor to remove the salt?

We suggest serving cod and salmon croquettes separately but at the same meal, mainly because of the interesting color contrast and also to offer diners a choice of flavors. We start out by wrapping large chunks of fresh cod and fresh salmon in cheese-

Chunks of cod and salmon, wrapped in cheesecloth to assist in lifting the chunks out intact, are covered with mirepoix and baked in vermouth.

cloth and poaching them in white wine flavored with basil or tarragon. The croquettes are serendipitous rewards from the leftovers.

Flake the two kinds of leftover fish separately and moisten the flakes with white wine. Then make a heavy white sauce of a flour-butter roux cooked with milk until thick and creamy. Salt to taste. Add the white sauce to the fish meat and mix well so that the mass is easily molded into cones or flat cakes, as desired. Dip the croquettes into beaten egg, roll in cracker or Wheaties crumbs, and then either pan- or deep fat-fry until golden.

FISH QUICHE   *Chenin Blanc*

Another excellent use for leftover fish is a variety of quiche not often seen. First, make a 9-inch pie shell of your favorite mix and bake 10 minutes in a 400-degree oven. To make the filling, you need:

3 eggs
1 cup half-and-half cream
½ tsp salt
1 cup flaked, cooked fish
1 cup shredded Swiss cheese
¼ cup chopped onion
⅛ tsp nutmeg
⅛ tsp cayenne
¼ cup chenin blanc

Combine the beaten eggs with all the other ingredients and pour into the partially baked pie shell. Sprinkle the top with cayenne. Bake in a 350-degree oven for about 45 minutes or until a silver knife comes out clean and the top is golden. Serve hot or cold, as preferred.

Quiche takes many forms, but this one is made from leftover meat from a whole baked fish.

CHAPTER 10

~~~~~~

Specialty Meats

Americans always have shown a great aversion to the specialty meats, very indelicately called "offal" in some European countries. Yet Americans will eat hot dogs by the ton, knowing very well what unspeakable trash they often contain. With tender loving care, the more unusual specialty items can be very delightful and delicious.

SAUERKRAUT AND KNOCKWURST   *Plum Wine*

Sauerkraut need not be the prototype of peasant dishes but can become a gourmet specialty with proper treatment. We find that plum wine and a few other touches give the necessary flair. While we suggest German knockwurst here, there is no reason not to use other German wursts, Polish kielbasa, Swedish sausage, or your choice.

Not really a company dish, Sauerkraut and Knockwurst in plum wine is excellent family fare, with its subtle juniper berry flavor.

1 lb sauerkraut, thoroughly rinsed and drained
1 knockwurst per person
   Bouillon and plum wine, mixed half and half
1 apple, peeled and quartered
1 tsp crushed juniper berries
3 tbsp cooking oil
3 onions, sliced

Sauté the onions and apple in the oil until softened. Add the sauerkraut and sauté 5 minutes more. Add the juniper berries and stir to mix well. Put the mixture into a casserole and add the bouillon-wine to barely cover. Place the sausages on top. Cover and braise in a 300-degree oven for 2 hours or more. Add more liquid if it cooks down too much.

SHERRIED CHICKEN LIVERS
ON ENGLISH MUFFINS
Sherry Amoroso

From all the chickens, cornish game hens, ducks, and turkeys, we accumulate the livers and freeze them. When a suitable quantity has been saved up, we revel in sherried livers on toasted English muffins at a Sunday breakfast.

> **4 livers per person**
> **Butter**
> ½ **cup Sherry Amoroso (see chapter 16)**
> **Salt and pepper**
> **Flour to dredge**
> **1 English muffin per person, split and toasted**

Trim the livers, dredge them in flour, and brown nicely on all sides in butter. Add the sherry and cook down, covered, until reduced by half. Salt and pepper to taste. Serve on the toasted muffins with the pan juice which has thickened during cooking, poured over as a sauce.

Chicken livers braised in sherry and served over English muffins make a highly satisfying and delicious breakfast or Sunday night supper.

SWEETBREADS MORNAY
IN PATTY SHELLS   *Sherry Amoroso*

 1 pair sweetbreads
 3 tbsp vinegar
 2 tbsp butter
 2 tbsp olive oil
   Leftover chicken meat
 1½ cups Bechamel sauce
 ½ cup shredded Swiss cheese
 2 tbsp Sherry Amoroso (see chapter 16)
 ½ cup mushroom buttons, sliced
   Toasted blanched sliced almonds
 2 tbsp capers of the dry salted type

Make the Bechamel sauce by adding equal parts of bouillon and milk to a white roux of flour and butter. A beaten egg yolk may be added to the sauce if desired but do not forget how to mix egg and a hot liquid! (See chapter 1.) Parboil the sweetbreads in water to cover with 3 tablespoons vinegar added. Drain and put into cold water until ready to use. Remove membrane from the sweetbreads and slice in ¼-inch pieces or break into small chunks. Sauté the sweetbreads in 2 tbsp butter and 2 tbsp olive oil with the mushrooms and cut-up chicken meat. Add to the Bechamel sauce and stir in most of the Swiss cheese. Add the sherry and capers and adjust the seasoning. Keep hot over a water bath for an hour to blend the flavors. Fill patty shells, and sprinkle with the remaining Swiss cheese and the toasted almond slivers. F ut under the broiler until the cheese is bubbly but do not burn the almonds.

BRAISED SWEETBREADS   *Tomato Wine*

Designated by such terrible terms as offal meat, innards, specialty meat, and other demeaning terms, sweetbreads have arisen from something given away or thrown away by most butchers, through a long exile as a women's luncheon dish in sloppy patty shells, to a more respectable position as a delicious dinner entree. Usually prepared with sherry, sweetbreads go well with tomato wine.

We are not partial to the bland à la king, cream-sauce-in-patty-shell style of cooking but we really like sweetbreads; so we came up with something different. Of course, we parboil the sweetbreads in vinegar water, remove the membranes, and make thin slices of the meat, which, if you care, is the thymus gland. Dredge the slices in flour and brown nicely on both sides in butter, adding salt and pepper. After the pieces are well browned, pour at least half a cup of tomato wine into the pan, cover, and simmer until the wine is reduced by half. Thicken the juices slightly with flour if desired and serve the sweetbreads on toast points with sauce over all.

Sweetbreads need not be confined to white sauce in a patty shell but can become a dinner entree when braised with wine.

BEEF AND KIDNEY PIE   *Zinfandel*

Probably the British will rush to do battle with us, pen in hand, as a result of our beef and kidney pie recipe but we simply answer with considerable assurance, "Yes, we know it is not traditional but it is delicious!" In fact, it is so delicious that we make the pies in individual baking dishes and keep a number on hand in the freezer at all times. We usually freeze them before they are baked.

Beef and Kidney Pie is so delicious that we keep several in the freezer at all times for spur-of-the-moment use.

1 lb lean, trimmed, stewing beef, cut in 1-inch cubes
Cooking oil
3 or 4 lamb kidneys
½ cup fresh mushrooms, sliced
½ cup chopped onion
2 crumbled bay leaves
½ tsp dry mustard
1 cup red wine
1 cup beef bouillon
Salt, pepper, paprika, and flour for dredging

First, wash the kidneys thoroughly and trim off all the white fibrous tissue. Then cut the kidneys into ¼-inch slices and cover them with red wine to marinate while other preparations are going forward. Dredge the beef cubes in flour containing salt, pepper, and paprika. Sauté the floured cubes in oil until nicely browned; then add the onion. Continue to sauté until the onion begins to brown and then add the mushrooms with the kidney slices, discarding the wine marinade. Add the seasonings, the bouillon, and the cup of wine, simmering for about an hour or until the beef is fork-tender. Remove the bay leaves at this time as they do not soften and are not agreeable to chew. Substitute bay leaf extract originally, if you prefer. Thicken the sauce if desired and adjust the seasoning. When cool, divide the mixture among individual baking dishes or ramekins and cover each with a top of slashed pastry. Bake the pies for 15 minutes at 450 degrees and then reduce heat to 250 degrees for another 20 minutes or until the pastry is done. This recipe makes 5 individual pies for us; it can also be baked in one large casserole. If you desire, this is a good recipe in which to use the popover mix or puff pastry top which we have described under Turkey Pot Pie in chapter 8.

REGAL LIVER AND ONIONS *Chianti*

Liver gets its bad name partly because it can taste strong or slightly bitter, but if you get slices of light brown calves' or pigs' liver instead of a slice of dark green-brown material from a steer or some poor old cow, you are off to a favorable start. Even if not a devotee of liver, you may find that wine makes the difference.

Select slices with few large white vessels or else do some trimming. Marinate the liver in chianti for at least an hour at room temperature. Then discard the marinade and pat the slices dry. Dredge in flour containing salt and pepper. Fry the slices on both sides in butter until browned and then add the sliced onions. Put in much more onion than you think necessary and then it will be about right. Continue to cook until the onions have softened and are transparent. Then about half-cover the meat with chianti and simmer, covered, stirring occasionally. Timing is inexact for this dish because of the wide variation in taste preferences as to the proper doneness of the liver. Prick with a fork until the juice has the color you like. By this time the wine will have reduced and will have thickened from the dredging flour.

Liver Parmigiana is only one of the several meats which emerge triumphantly from the parmigiana treatment with tomato sauce and cheeses.

LIVER PARMIGIANA　　　　　　　　　　　*Cabernet*

The liver taste is masked nicely by the parmigiana process and the dish is highly tasty. Select slices of young liver and trim off the blood vessels. Marinate the liver for at least an hour in red wine and then discard the marinade. Pat the slices dry; dip them in beaten egg and then in seasoned crumbs with salt and pepper. Sauté the meat until the juice is barely pink. Arrange the liver in individual au gratin dishes or one large casserole and bake for 30 minutes in a 325-degree oven. Now cover the meat with Italian tomato sauce, used liberally. Cover all with slices of mozzarella cheese and a thick sprinkling of grated parmesan cheese. Bake 15 minutes longer or until the cheese is melted and the sauce is bubbly.

BRAISED HARE　　　　　　　　　　　*Rose Hip Wine*

Well, all right! So it is fried rabbit but you must admit that "braised hare" makes it sound more interesting and exotic. Use whatever pieces are available or preferred, allowing about half a small rabbit per person. Wash the pieces carefully and even though the rabbit may have been hutch-raised, be very careful not to prick a finger on a bone fragment.

Dredge the pieces of meat in seasoned flour and then brown them nicely on all sides, using cooking oil in a casserole or iron skillet. Now add about 2 cups of rose hip wine or enough to half-cover the meat. Braise covered in a 350-degree oven for about 1½ hours or until the meat is fork-tender. Thicken the pan juices for a delicious sauce. Serve with simply prepared vegetables such as boiled potatoes, parsnips, or carrots, cooked in bouillon, not water.

STUFFED BEEF HEART   *Red Wine*

Beef hearts are not easy to come by but the difficulty in finding them is offset by the end result. The meat is quite firm, not unlike flank steak, and lends itself to similar treatment. First, trim off all the white blood vessels at the base of the heart and then reach into both cavities, pulling and cutting out as much as possible of the membranous valve tissue.

The heart may be stuffed with whatever dressing you prefer but the bread-cube, sage dressing discussed under Stuffings for Fowl in chapter 8 is traditional and delicious. Here, soak the bread in red wine to complement the meat. Then stuff the heart as tightly as possible. Place it in a pan with 2 cups of red wine and bake at 350 degrees for 1½ hours. The meat always is quite firm; so longer cooking is acceptable and fork-testing is not reliable. Slice to serve.

SPICED TONGUE   *Red Wine*

Calf or beef tongue should be marinated overnight at room temperature in a half wine-half vinegar marinade containing thyme, sage, and mashed juniper berries. The next day, pat the tongue dry and put it in a kettle, covering with half bouillon-half red wine. Add the same type spices as those used in the marinade plus 2 crumbled hot red peppers. Bring this to a boil and simmer for 2 hours, even if the tongue is of the smoked rather than the fresh variety. If a pressure cooker is used, it will be done in about half the time. Allow to cool and "peel" the tongue, removing the very rough skin. The tongue usually is served cold in sandwiches, in chunks in tossed salad, or however cold cuts are used.

CALVES' BRAINS   *Chablis*

Calves' brains are delicious but very soft and difficult to handle. It is best to boil them whole before trying to remove the membranes, lest they go to pieces irretrievably. We usually boil a set of brains for 20 minutes in half bouillon-half white wine and, when cool, proceed with the removal of membranes and blood vessels. By this time the brain tissue will have become solid enough to hold its shape. The secret of success is to weigh a half-brain down with a plate and a pan of water so it will flatten out into a sheet.

For brains and black butter, heavily flour the brain sheets, sauté them until nicely browned in butter, remove them, and cook the juices at high heat until the butter begins to darken. Add a tablespoon of capers and lemon juice and heat through. Place the brains on a heated plate and pour the black butter over all.

A delicious breakfast or brunch dish is made by cutting the bouillon-wine-cooked brains into small pieces and, using the proportion of 3 eggs to ½ cup of brains, scrambling the mixture. Serve on toast points.

Finally, try substituting diced wine-bouillon-cooked brains for sweetbreads or chicken in patty shells.

~~~~~~

CHAPTER 11

Treats from the Barbecue Grill

There is no reason, unless the entire family is made up of adolescents, why the barbecue grill should be restricted to hamburgers and hot dogs. Hamburgers are a fat, deadly bore and hot dogs contain things which even dogs should not be expected to eat. So much for national mores! The patio grill is a lot of fun and can be a source of gourmet pleasure for adults as well as for kids, using a little imagination.

BARBECUED LONG ISLAND DUCKLING *Orange-Cranberry Wine*

Long Island duckling is excellent roasted on the indoor rotisserie or baked in the ordinary or microwave oven, as well as barbecued alfresco with more flair. There is nothing more stimulating to the flow of digestive juices than to sit around the patio quaffing a tall drink while watching dinner revolve as it assumes a golden brown patina. Second best, roasted indoors, the duckling becomes a year-around festive dish.

Duckling traditionally is served with an orange sauce but any one of a number of fruit wine flavors is highly acceptable. We have adapted a number of homemade wines in various sauces to be served over this roasted bird. These tend to be sweet sauces, for which duck has an affinity. Fortunately, duck accepts hot-sour barbecue sauces with equal grace, and we make several of these with wine also. Use your own choice, but here we use orange-cranberry wine sauce.

Our basic sweet wine sauce for duckling is the same as the one we use for Mulberry Hasty Pudding or other desserts (see Fruit Wine Dessert Sauce in chapter 13). In this case we make the sauce with Orange-Cranberry Wine (see chapter 16). Heat the sauce until thick and clear. Serve separately with the duckling.

For a hot-sour sauce to serve with the duckling or other roast, we use:

Barbecued Long Island Duckling needs to be trussed carefully and mounted on the spit accurately so it will turn evenly and regularly. The bed of coals should be red covered by gray.

A near-black, crisp, delicious edible skin results from periodic painting of the skin with marinade. We serve one duck for two persons, just cutting the duck in two with fowl shears.

⅓ cup chutney (peach, pear, quince, or your choice)
½ **cup red wine**
2 tbsp tarragon vinegar
3 tsp horseradish
¼ tsp cayenne (or to your taste)

Our favorite barbecue sauce for marinade, basting, or to surround poultry and other roasts, when the meat is to be roasted indoors rather than over charcoal heat, is:

½ **cup lemon juice**
¼ **cup tomato catsup**
1 tsp dried red pepper
10 drops lemon oil or peel of 1 lemon, grated
Chives, a crumbled handful
1 cup red wine

Choose a 4- to 6-pound bird. Rub it inside and out with salt and black pepper. Truss the bird snugly with heavy twine which will not immediately burn off. Spit the duckling so that it will revolve evenly. Start a sparse charcoal fire at least 30 minutes before using. When the ash is red-gray, put the spit in place and start it revolving. Remember to make a small fire unless you want to incinerate rather than barbecue. The turning bird bastes in its own melting fat, and your main function is to act as a firefighter, with a bulb to mist water if needed.

It is difficult to predict the time of readiness, evidenced by the juices dripping clear and yellow instead of red or pink. Variations in cooking time depend on size of fire, size of bird, and the velocity and direction of wind. Just keep the guests entertained until all is ready.

Since ducklings of 4 to 6 pounds serve only 2 persons, we just split the bird down the middle with fowl shears and make no attempt at carving. If you basted with barbecue sauce during roasting, the skin will be brown-black but highly edible. If you did not baste with the barbecue sauce, serve with the orange-cranberry wine sauce or use the same recipe, substituting any preferred fruit wine. Be sure to salvage some nice chunks of meat to freeze for the next casserole of cassoulet.

HICKORY-BROILED STEAK
WITH WINE MARINADE   *Cabernet*

T-bone, club, shell, or other 2-inch steaks of your choice really do not need wine and actually are excellent when grilled over charcoal, even without hickory chips, but the addition of wine and hickory smoke gilds the lily very creditably. Steaks can be marinated in anything up to and including bourbon or gin, but we find red wine sufficient if we want a subtle taste change. Marinating for an hour at room temperature is enough for a tender steak.

Start the charcoal fire at least a half-hour ahead of time and relax with a martini. Rushing things is no real help. When the coals are red, covered with gray, elevate the grill to its highest point, put some water-soaked hickory slivers on the glowing

Hickory-broiled Steak with Wine Marinade is best when cooked rare, in our opinion. Black outside and red inside! When the hickory slivers finish smoldering, they go up in flame, as seen here.

coals, and put the steaks on the grill. Turn once or twice. The marvelously fragrant smoke will be gone in 5 to 10 minutes. Then lower the grill to cooking level, proceeding with the rite and hopefully ending with a steak charred somewhat on the outside and delightfully red and juicy on the inside, with that overall hickory flavor. No steak sauce is needed with this, only salt and pepper.

DOUBLE-THICK PORK CHOPS
WITH WINE SAUCE
Peach Wine

We prepare double-thick pork chops by the shake-and-bake method during the winter months but in the barbecue season, we like to hickory-smoke-broil them on the grill along with grilled corn on the cob. The chops should be at least 1½ inches thick. The coals-smoke routine is the same as for steak in the preceding recipe, but the chops must be cooked very well done. When the juices become pale pink, we put husked sweet corn all around the edges, repeatedly brushing the ears with melted butter. A few passes with the butter brush over the chops is not amiss at this juncture. We let the corn sizzle and pop, even turning dark brown in places; meantime, the chops become crusted and well-done. We serve them with our Fruit Wine Dessert Sauce, described in chapter 13. That made with peach wine is a favorite.

Double-thick Pork Chops with Wine Sauce are grilled to complete doneness with a black-brown crust but a juicy inside. We husk the corn completely and roast it bare with frequent brushings of melted butter.

GRILLED CHICKEN QUARTERS   *Vermouth*

Chicken is very toothsome, almost no matter how prepared, if it is cooked past the pink "slick" stage. Very subtle changes in seasoning form the basis for all sorts of delectable treats. At a Mediterranean restaurant we once had a whole roast chicken brought to the table and flamed over laurel smoke from a charcoal brazier. This made quite an impression on us and, realizing that bay leaf flavor comes from European laurel bushes, we figured out how to arrive at the same delicious end.

We use quartered chickens, two pieces per person, and broil them over the charcoal grill by the ordinary technique except that we marinate the chicken first in vermouth to which we have added a tablespoon of bay leaf extract. After marinating for an hour or more, place the dripping pieces over the coals. As the chicken cooks, continue to brush the marinade over it very frequently. The aroma is great. Probably, bay leaf extract could be drizzled onto the coals at intervals with even greater effect, although we have not tried it as yet. The chicken is unique.

Chicken quarters may not only be marinated with vermouth flavored with bay leaf extract before grilling, but may be brushed liberally and often with bay leaf extract to produce a very Mediterranean dish.

Medium-sized lobster tails are grilled until the meat is firm and opaque while the cleared juices bubble in the joints.

GRILLED LOBSTER TAILS
WITH WINE SAUCE   *Red Wine*

Lobster tails come in all sizes from near-shrimp to four or more pounds, depending on the species and region of origin. The clawless "lobsters" of the tropics really are crayfish, but no matter, they are delicious. We like to get the huge lobster tails, which we split once lengthwise and once crosswise to give four monstrous servings. Of necessity, these are grilled out of the shell and painted liberally from time to time with lemon butter. The meat is done when it is firm, opaque, and has clear juice exuding. The smaller tails we leave in the shell, removing only the under-parts with shears. These are done when the juice in the joints bubbles clear. Addition of hickory chips to the charcoal bed is very tasty and provides an unusual touch. We serve the tails with our B-2 Sauce, since someone else has patented an A-1 sauce. This recipe is given in chapter 13.

GRILLED STEAK TERIYAKI   *Sherry Amoroso*

The Japanese are past-masters at grilling over a charcoal hibachi, and the second- or third-generation Japanese-American citizens of the Hawaiian Islands have kept up the tradition. Almost any kind of meat can be cut into narrow strips, threaded onto bamboo splinters, and grilled over charcoal. Chicken teriyaki is excellent, but we prefer the beef variety. Prior marinating adds distinctive flavor.

First, make teriyaki sauce, which can be refrigerated or frozen. This simply is equal parts of dry sherry wine, soy sauce, and chicken bouillon. To make the teriyaki glaze, use

    ¼ **cup teriyaki sauce**
    1 tbsp sugar
    2 tbsp cornstarch in 1 tbsp sherry

Steak teriyaki may be grilled on small skewers over a brazier as an hors d'oeuvre or on long skewers, as here, being unskewered onto a bed of fluffy rice as an entree.

Cook at low heat until the glaze is thick and clear. Cut lean tenderloin or sirloin into ¼-inch strips and thread these onto bamboo slivers (skewers), pushing the beef toward one end. Dip each piece of skewered meat into the glaze and broil over a charcoal bed for about a minute on each side. Broil an additional minute for well done. This is a cocktail buffet preparation which each guest cooks for himself; but for an entree, use long metal skewers and bigger pieces of meat and broil many at once. To serve, unskewer onto a bed of rice and pass hot glaze separately.

ROYAL HAMBURGERS *Zinfandel*

We cast disdainful glances at hamburgers mainly because they are so mundane and ubiquitous. When treated with a little flair, however, they certainly have their place. The texture of hamburgers is much improved by working into the ground meat as much red wine as it will take. This amounts to not over 15 percent by weight. Any excess will not be absorbed or else it simply boils out and drips onto the charcoal bed. Addition of a few hickory chips to the coals certainly does not detract from the flavor. We would not think of saying how long to broil hamburgers because tastes vary. Only remember that moist meat takes a little longer.

LONDON BROIL WITH
CURRY-WINE STEAK SAUCE *Red Wine*

We have described the pinwheel pieces of flank steak or the thick chunks of top round, both broiled and both called London broil (see chapter 4). Either style can be cooked to great advantage over the charcoal grill, especially with provision for hickory smoke. This particular preparation is especially good with Curry-Wine Steak Sauce, described in chapter 13. Leftovers are excellent sliced thin in open-faced luncheon sandwiches or ground to make a forcemeat for stuffing green peppers.

BREAST OF CHICKEN EN BROCHETTE *Chianti*

All of the countries in which cooking is customarily done over charcoal braziers have an extensive cuisine of skewered items because this is a convenient way to manage small pieces of meat. Usually, such countries feature bite-sized pieces of meat; so these two points go together nicely. Skewer cooking can be limited to the outdoor grill but modern conveniences allow it all year, using the indoor oven and a skewer rack. All of the following skewer recipes are equally applicable to indoor or outdoor use. Plan on one skewer per person.

Cubes of chicken breast meat
Chicken livers
Whole fresh mushrooms
Homemade sausage balls (see Pork Sausage)
Chianti
Allspice
Salt and pepper

Skewered meats should be those which cook rapidly, as chicken, shown here alternating with chicken livers and mushrooms. Alternate skewers contain Shrimp en Brochette.

Using about ½ teaspoon of allspice per cup of chianti, marinate the chicken cubes, livers, mushrooms, and sausage balls for several hours at room temperature. Then lightly salt and pepper all the items and spit them alternately on long skewers. With the charcoal fire started at least a half-hour previously and now reduced to gray ash over red coals, put the skewers on a frame over the source of heat. Rotate the skewers periodically until the food is done as evidenced by the exuding of yellow rather than pink juices or bloody fluid. Unskewer over fluffy rice.

Here, some skewers hold Lamb Shashlik while the alternate ones hold scallops. This allows for some taste preference among guests.

LAMB SHASHLIK
Quince Wine

Marinate cubes of lamb in quince wine containing ½ teaspoon of rosemary per cup of wine for several hours at room temperature. On long skewers, alternate lamb chunks, chunks of thick-cut bacon, and small, partly cooked potatoes. Broil over charcoal or in the oven, making sure that the bacon is well done. The marinade may be thickened with cornstarch as a sauce.

SCALLOPS EN BROCHETTE   *Vermouth*

Marinate for several hours at room temperature large scallops in vermouth containing 1 teaspoon of bay leaf extract per cup of wine. Dredge the scallops in flour and sauté them until nearly done. Then skewer the scallops, with a skewered bay leaf between each scallop. Broil until hot through. Thicken the marinade as a sauce.

BEEF-KIDNEY SHISH KEBAB   *Zinfandel*

Trim lamb kidneys and parboil them in half bouillon-half red wine. Cut the kidneys into large chunks. Trim lean tenderloin of sirloin into cubes. Marinate the beef and kidneys for several hours at room temperature in zinfandel containing ½ teaspoon oregano per cup of wine. On a long skewer, alternately spear beef cubes, kidney chunks, and canned small white onions. Broil until the beef has cooked to the desired degree and the other items are hot through. Discard the marinade.

This beef-kidney-mushroom skewer is a version of beef-kidney pie and just as good.

SHRIMP EN BROCHETTE   *Chenin Blanc*

Shrimp deserve the best and we favor giving it to them! Marinate large, deveined shrimp in chenin blanc containing a teaspoon of tarragon per cup of wine for several hours at room temperature. On long skewers, alternately mount shrimp, pineapple chunks, and chunks of cooked ham. Broil until the shrimp are opaque, pink, and obviously done. Unskewer over fluffy rice, using the thickened marinade as a sauce.

Few entrees can rival the reef and beef combo of lobster tails and sirloin steak. Wine marinades add extra interest and piquancy.

LOBSTER-STEAK COMBO   *Red and White Wine*

While we were living in Hawaii, some twelve years ago, a Waikiki restaurant began serving a lobster tail-sirloin steak combination which attained instant popularity. Tourists quickly made the idea their own and soon introduced it to home-town restaurants far and wide under various names such as Surf and

Turf or Beef and Reef. Whether broiled indoors in the oven or outdoors over charcoal, this marriage of sea and meadow is excellent. We usually marinate the beef in red wine and the lobster tails in white wine for several hours at room temperature. Various simply made wine sauces (see chapter 13) add piquancy and special tang.

1 nice piece of tenderloin or sirloin per person
1 medium to large lobster tail per person
Red and white wines

This festive dish is extremely easy to prepare but rates high on the gourmet list. Just grill the marinated meats over a hickory-smoke barbecue grill until the juices from the lobster tails boil in the joints and the meat is opaque and firm. We do the steak rare, but take your choice. Serve on heated plates with baked potato and chive-sour cream dressing. Pass the wine sauces separately.

CHAPTER 12

~~~~~~

Eggs and Cheese

What we would do without eggs and cheese as adjuncts in cooking is difficult to conceive, but occasionally these versatile delicacies really stand on their own feet as the center of attraction in a gourmet recipe. Many recipes using these ingredients appear in previous chapters, but there are some really great ones yet to mention.

SERENDIPITOUS OMELETTES

There are essentially two types of omelettes. One is the French "shake" type made in a large slope-wall pan in which the eggs are shaken with a push-pull motion, forming them into a loose roll as the eggs cook. Such an omelette does not readily lend itself to filling because it does not sit still long enough, but various meat, cheese, fish, mushroom, and other sauces can be poured over it.

Serendipitous omelettes are made with fillings of our favorite pâtés: cheese, chicken liver, and shrimp. The hinged pan lends itself to filled omelettes better than the slope-sided "push-pull" French pan.

The other omelette, an imposter in the eyes of purists, is made in a hinged pan. Both halves are filled with eggs beaten with a little cream; after some cooking, a filling is placed on top of one layer in the pan, which then is closed. Thus, the filling ends up in the middle and the pan can be flipped over to cook both sides of the omelette. There is some justification for insisting that this creation really is a soufflé rather than an omelette, but this is the type we make for Sunday breakfast, brunch, lunch, or late supper. Our three main pâtés—chicken liver, shrimp, and Cheese Jar (see chapter 2)—are excellent fillings. Our pan accommodates a 3-egg omelette very nicely. As with any soufflé, time quickly wrecks the creation; so be prepared to eat at once! Any delay gives the chef gray hairs.

SWISS CHEESE FONDUE
*Apple Wine and
Black Cherry Liqueur*

Swiss cheese fondue is famous as an after-ski-party dinner, but even after nothing more strenuous than a tough session at the TV watching some young men maim each other, Swiss fondue is an agreeable and filling meal. For a Sunday night supper it cannot be surpassed.

We use so much Swiss cheese in cooking that we buy it several pounds at a time, put it through the fine cone of the food shredder, and then freeze it in plastic bags. This is very convenient for sprinkling grated cheese on various oven or casserole dishes and is especially helpful in making fondue which calls for grated Swiss cheese by the cupful. Here is how to make fondue, quantities being listed per person.

> **2 cups shredded Swiss cheese, preferably imported**
> ½ **cup apple wine**
> **Dash of nutmeg**
> ¼ **tsp garlic chips or garlic powder**
> 1 **tbsp cornstarch**
> 2 **tbsp Cherry Heering or kirsch**

Add the nutmeg and garlic chips or powder to the wine, heat over a double boiler, and then add the cheese. Stir until com-

Swiss Cheese Fondue is particularly good as a Sunday night supper or an after-sport party dish.

This is Chili con Queso, which differs from a fondue mainly by being a little thinner in consistency and being used as a dip for tortilla segments.

pletely melted and ropy. Then stir in the cornstarch dissolved in the liqueur. (Instead of the Cherry Heering or kirsch, you may substitute calvados or one of the orange-flavored liqueurs.) Continue stirring until entirely blended and smooth. Meantime, heat a French or Italian hard roll per person and cut into bite-sized cubes, each with crust on one side. Bring the double boiler to the table and set it in the center. Serve with long-handled fondue forks, a tossed salad, fruit, coffee, and a liqueur. Remember to spear and dip carefully because whoever loses a piece of bread into the pot must pay a forfeit. If there is any left-over fondue, it can be warmed up for a second go-around later. It also makes an excellent omelette filling and, spread on Triscuits and broiled until bubbly, it is a delicious hors d'oeuvre.

CHEDDAR CHEESE FONDUE   *Cabernet*

Much more robust in flavor than Swiss Cheese Fondue, the cheddar dish could almost be mistaken for Chili con Queso (see chapter 2) except that the fondue is served as an entree rather than an hors d'oeuvre and it is less spicy. Per person you need:

> **2 cups very sharp cheddar cheese, shredded**
> **½ cup red wine**
> **1 tbsp cornstarch in 2 tbsp wine**
> **½ tsp garlic chips**
> **¼ tsp tarragon**
> **¼ tsp cayenne**

Use the same procedure as for the preceding recipe and serve in the same way. Leftovers may be used in the same ways, too.

WELSH RAREBIT   *Chianti*

Whether billed as rabbit or rarebit and whether attributable to the Welsh or to 100 other nationalities, this cheddar dish is a favorite in many regions. Basically, the dish is melted cheddar cheese with ale, mustard, and a bit of some hot sauce. The simplest form is to lay a slice of cheese on a slice of bread, spread on some mustard, and toast it until bubbly. We bypass the exotic ingredients except to remind the reader that melted cheddar on toast with a piece of grilled bacon and tomato on top is a good dish. For rarebit, we use per person:

> **3 cups very sharp cheddar cheese, shredded**
> **2 tbsp butter**
> **1 tsp hot mustard**
> **1 tsp worcestershire sauce**
> **½ cup chianti**
> **2 egg yolks, beaten**
> **Paprika**

In a double boiler, heat the wine and add all the other ingredients except the egg yolks. When the cheese has melted and the mixture is smooth, but not yet blended, stir in the beaten egg yolks, beating rapidly. Keep hot and serve over hot toast with a sprinkle of paprika on top for looks.

CHAPTER 13

~~~~~~

Sauces and Salad Dressings

$\mathbf{S}$auces and dressings add that subtle touch which merits an extra star or two for some otherwise quite pedestrian dish. If you get into the habit of thinking about sauces, there is no end to those which you can devise and really no end to the ways in which you can embellish the time-honored stand-bys. Wine often does the trick.

CHINESE SAUCE   *Sherry*

The bite-sized pieces of meat, no matter of what type, used in Chinese dishes, usually are marinated in a mixture combining sherry wine, soy sauce, and other ingredients. An example of such sauce good with fish, fowl, or beef is:

2 tbsp sherry or rice wine
3 tbsp soy sauce
1 tbsp cornstarch
¾ tsp salt
¼ tsp chopped fresh ginger
¼ tsp crushed garlic

For a more basic marinade, just omit the ginger and garlic.

MUSHROOM WINE SAUCE   *Red or White Wine*

1 cup red or white wine
½ cup bouillon
1 tbsp butter
½ cup chopped mushrooms
2 tbsp cornstarch in 2 tbsp wine

Simmer the mushrooms in the wine-bouillon-butter until done. Add the cornstarch, stirring vigorously. If desired, add chopped shallots and chopped chives.

B-2 BARBECUE SAUCE   *Red Wine*

2 tbsp peach, pear, or mango chutney
½ cup red wine
1 tbsp tarragon vinegar
3 tsp grated horseradish
¼ tsp cayenne

Useful with any meat, especially London broil.

LEMON SAUCE FOR LONDON BROIL   *Red Wine*

½ cup lemon juice
¼ cup tomato puree
1 tsp dried red pepper
   Peel of one lemon, grated
   Chives, a handful, chopped fine
1 cup red wine

CURRY-WINE STEAK SAUCE *Red Wine*

To the lemon sauce above, add:

1 tbsp curry powder
¼ cup olive oil
1 tsp salt
Black pepper as desired

Mix well and shake before using. You might substitute 1 tablespoon chili powder instead of the curry, for variety.

BARBECUE SAUCE *Red Wine*

We stumbled onto our favorite barbecue sauce by misreading a recipe. The recipe called for a slice of lemon and we thought it said one lemon, sliced! The result was so delicious that we have continued to make this mistake for about 15 years now.

½ cup tarragon vinegar
1 cup red wine
4 tbsp sugar
2 tbsp hot mustard
1 tsp black pepper
3 tsp salt
½ tsp cayenne
1 lemon, sliced thin
2 sliced onions
½ cup butter
2 cups tomato catsup
4 tbsp worcestershire sauce

Simmer all the ingredients about 10 minutes.

RÉMOULADE *Red Wine*

This is excellent as a spread on sandwich bread, substituting for mayonnaise. It is great on cold meats and, diluted with some wine, it is a tasty filling for an avocado cavity as a salad. There are many recipes for rémoulade, most of which in no way resemble each other. Here is our version.

> 1 raw egg
> 2 hard-boiled eggs
> ⅓ cup tarragon vinegar
> ⅓ cup red wine
> ½ cup cooking oil
> ½ tsp garlic salt
> 1½ tsp horseradish
> 2 tbsp tomato catsup
> 2½ tbsp hot paprika
> 1 tsp cayenne
> ½ cup green onions with tops
> ⅓ cup hot mustard

Blend all the ingredients at high speed and gradually add enough bread crumbs to thicken to a mayonnaise consistency. This sauce keeps well and freezes perfectly.

SHERRY SAUCE

Originally for use with turkey, this sauce is equally good with chicken or baked fish. It freezes well.

In a double boiler, heat 1 cup of chicken bouillon, 1 cup of heavy cream, and ¼ cup sherry. Heat not quite to boiling. Pour a little at a time into 4 beaten egg yolks, beating constantly. Return to the double boiler and cook until the sauce coats a spoon, stirring frequently. Remove from heat and stir in salt, white pepper, and lemon juice to taste. More sherry may be added if desired.

An interesting variation is to substitute orange-cranberry wine for the sherry, making a seasonal complement for the holiday bird.

JAVANESE PEANUT SAUCE   *Red Grape Wine*

For pork or chicken, this piquant sauce cannot be beat. It freezes well and can be served either hot or cold.

1 small onion, chopped
¼ tsp ground cardamom
¼ cup packed brown sugar
¼ cup lemon juice
¼ tsp ground coriander
2 tbsp peanut or cooking oil
½ cup chunky peanut butter
¼ cup soy sauce
¼ tsp red pepper seasoning
½ cup red wine

Sauté the onion in the oil and stir in the cardamom. Cool slightly. Blend the peanut butter and the brown sugar in a small bowl and then stir in the remaining ingredients, adding the cooled onion last. Thin with a half-cup of bouillon. Just bring to a simmer if the sauce is to be served with hot meat or refrigerate if for cold.

HOT-SOUR WINE SAUCE
FOR RED MEAT   *Red Wine*

For hot-sour sauce to serve with red meat, we use:

⅓ cup pear, peach, or quince chutney
½ cup red wine
2 tbsp tarragon vinegar
3 tsp horseradish, grated or prepared
¼ tsp cayenne, or to taste

For use with fish or fowl, we substitute a white fruit wine in place of the red wine. We do not use this sauce for marinade or basting but only served separately at table.

TRADITIONAL ORANGE SAUCE
FOR DUCKLING   *White Wine*

For the traditional orange flavor, boil half a cup of dry white wine down to about ⅓ cup and add 2 tablespoons orange liqueur. Stir in a teaspoon of cornstarch, stirring constantly until the sauce is clear and of the desired thickness. Cherry sauce is made in the same way, substituting Cherry Heering for the orange liqueur. Another excellent choice is raspberry sauce, made in the same way with raspberry liqueur. For extra eye appeal, appropriately add slivers of orange peel, some halved black cherries, or a tablespoon of raspberry jam.

SALAD DRESSING   *Red or White Wine*

The customary oil-vinegar dressing calls for 2 parts oil and 1 part vinegar, but since we do not need the extra calories, we make it with 1 part olive or cooking oil, 1 part red or white wine, and 1 part vinegar, with salt and black pepper to taste.

We make a very favorite curry-hot salad dressing from the 1 part oil, 1 part wine, 1 part vinegar (or lemon juice) base by adding 2 teaspoons dehydrated onion chips and 1 teaspoon hot curry powder. The onion takes up the liquids without the necessity of prior soaking in water.

For fruit salad, if you are going to thin the mayonnaise, use wine of a complementary flavor or one of the herb wines such as lemon balm, angelica, or tarragon. Fruit salad or a mixed fruit plate profits by a French dressing with liqueur added to taste, as a sweet-sour dressing. Here again, a fruit flavor may be chosen, but the spice-herb taste of benedictine is delicious. An eye-appealing, taste-tickling gelatin salad is made with black cherry jello, using the juice from a no. 2 can of black cherries as part of the liquid. When the jello begins to set, add the pitted, halved black cherries, a cup of chopped celery, half a cup of walnuts, and half a cup of sliced pimento-stuffed olives. Put into a ring or individual molds. Serve on lettuce bed with a dressing, prepared as follows, drizzled over or served separately. Thin heavy mayonnaise with Cherry Heering or be venturesome and try the almond flavor of crème de noyaux. Actually, your favorite liqueur is worth a try.

FRUIT WINE DESSERT SAUCE

For puddings or over ice cream, try the following:

1 cup fruit wine, reduced to ¾ cup by boiling
1 tbsp sugar
1 tbsp butter
2 tsp cornstarch in 2 tbsp wine

Any of the fruit wines do well in this sauce. We choose either a similar or a contrasting flavor and sometimes choose for the color, such as raspberry.

WALDORF SALAD   *Crème de Cacao*

Waldorf salad seems to have slipped from popularity, an entirely undeserved fate. Use firm, red, unpeeled apples, cored and chopped coarsely. Per half-cup of apple, use half a cup of chopped celery and ¼ cup of walnut meats. For the salad dressing, use heavy whipped cream thinned with an added liqueur to light mayonnaise consistency. Crème de cacao is an excellent choice or you may prefer a contrasting fruit-flavored liqueur or one of the spice-herb types such as strega.

~~~~~~

CHAPTER 14

Desserts
with Wines and Liqueurs

One beauty of making dry wines is that while they are just right for general cooking purposes, they can be sweetened very easily for use in desserts. Sometimes in fruit-based desserts we use the same kind of wine as the dessert fruit to reinforce the flavor, but a contrasting or complementing flavor adds extra interest. In all of the desserts which we recommend, any fruit of the season or region can be substituted for something which is not available. Also, fruit wines and fruit-flavored liqueurs can be used interchangeably, with the liqueurs giving sweeter results.

Everyone knows of the delights of an after-dinner liqueur; many realize that as a frappé over crushed ice, most liqueurs are delicious; a small number of people are acquainted with the various liqueurs in coffee as café royal, but almost no one knows of the many ways in which liqueurs can be used in gourmet recipes. The cordials, of course, are too sweet for general use in cooking, but their bright colors and interesting

Dry wines can easily be converted to sweet wines for use in many ways in sauces and desserts.

flavors really bring them into prominence in desserts, where they are extremely useful. Even the more exotic herb flavors can be very welcome additions.

TIPS ON FRUIT TARTS

Piecrust becomes an excellent tart dough with the simple substitution of a liqueur for the required pie-dough liquid. A little added shortening makes a richer tart dough which can actually be baked as cookies. To make a tart shell, use your choice of liqueur in the mix; roll out a little thicker than usual or press the dough into a pie tin. Set in another pie tin or use foil and dry beans to fill the shell while baking to prevent the dough from slipping down. These tart shells can be used in many ways, as we will show you.

BLUE PLUM TART   *Plum Wine*

About 20 fresh, ripe Italian prune plums
1 cup plum wine
1 cup water
3 tbsp plum heart liqueur
3 tbsp quick-cooking tapioca

Cut plums in half and remove seeds, reserving the seeds to make more plum heart liqueur. Bring the plum halves to boil in the water, wine, and liqueur. Simmer for 1 minute and, with a slotted spoon, carefully remove the plum halves to a cooky sheet to cool. Add the tapioca to the cooking liquid and, stirring constantly, cook over low heat 6 to 8 minutes until the mixture is clear and thickened. Set it aside.

Make your favorite 8-inch pie or tart crust, substituting plum wine for the liquid. Line a removable-bottom tart form by pressing in the dough. Put foil over the crust, extending over the edges, and fill the pan with dry beans, to prevent the bottom from buckling. Bake the crust in a 375-degree oven for 10 to 12

Four-compartment bottles permit the keeping of a large variety of liqueurs handy for after-dinner choice or for wide use in desserts.

minutes; then remove the foil and beans, continuing to bake until the crust is golden brown. Let it cool and then arrange the plum halves in the tart shell in a single layer, using your ingenuity as a pattern. For example, concentric circles alternating plums with cut side up and cut side down is pleasing. Spoon the thickened liquid over the plums so all the plums and the crust are well coated. Return to the oven for 10 minutes. Cool before serving.

The Italian blue prune plum makes a colorful and delicious tart in which plum wine and plum liqueur, flavored with the bitter-almond taste of the seeds, take their place.

With the blue plum tart as a prototype, there is literally no end to the types of fruit tarts and combinations of fruits. Using variations in the wine and liqueur opens up infinite possibilities. We heartily recommend apple, peach, plum, pear, strawberry, raspberry, mango, nectarine, pineapple, and banana. Some of the canned fruits such as apricot are especially good. Be sure to try to make the tart a work of art as well as a culinary triumph. For example, use banana wine and pineapple liqueur, placing long slices of raw ripe banana dipped in lemon juice in a radial pattern with fresh or canned pineapple triangles in between. Even some of the more exotic tarts are good, such as rhubarb and strawberry; or try ripe gooseberries decorated with large green gooseberries for a filling. When in doubt as to what wine to use, always fall back on sherry—or just close your eyes and grab one!

DEEP DISH APPLE PIE   *Apple Wine*

Every American is addicted to apple pie or so the sayings go, but few know the real pleasure of apple wine deep dish apple pie. For this extraordinary dish, use a 2-quart casserole. Peel, core, quarter, and slice 5 or 6 apples into the casserole and over their surface sprinkle ¾ cup of sugar, 1 teaspoon ground cinnamon, and 2 tablespoons flour. Dot with butter and pour ½ cup apple wine over all. Cover the dish with your favorite piecrust dough, using apple wine for the liquid. Roll the dough a little thicker than usual and prick it generously to prevent the juices from boiling over. Bake the pie for 30 to 35 minutes in a 375-degree oven and wait until mealtime to try it, if you can. It is delicious cold with whipped cream or ice cream. Other deep dish fruit pies will come to mind with a little thought about it.

APPLE DUMPLING   *Apple Wine*

Apple dumpling is a prototype; so any other fruit can be used with slight modifications which will become apparent. Apple dumpling is sheathed in your favorite rich biscuit, shortcake, or pie dough, with apple wine substituted for the liquid called for in the recipe. Make the dough into 6-inch diameter circles. Carefully peel and core an apple, leaving the bottom intact and unbroken. Place the apple at the center of a dough circle and fill the cavity with apple wine. Over the apple, sprinkle about 2 tablespoons sugar, 1 teaspoon flour, some ground cinnamon, and a few dots of

Apple dumpling is a he-man-sized dessert, good either hot or cold. It freezes well even with the wine sauce on it.

butter. Moisten the edges of the dough, close it all around the apple, and crimp the edges tight. Bake the dumpling about 45 minutes in a 350-degree oven or until golden brown. Serve the dumpling either hot or cold with the Fruit Wine Dessert Sauce described in the preceding chapter. The dumpling will freeze well either baked or uncooked. If baked, it can be frozen with the sauce on it.

MANDARIN MARMALADE PIE   *Orange Liqueur*

An exotic pie which will remind you somewhat of pecan pie in appearance is Mandarin Marmalade Pie, using either oranges, mandarin oranges, or tangerines. To make it, you need:

2 oranges
1¼ cups sugar
Juice of ½ lemon
2½ tbsp cornstarch
¼ cup softened butter
½ cup plus 1 tsp water
3 eggs
2 tbsp orange liqueur
Pastry for a 2-crust pie

With a vegetable peeler, remove paper-thin slices of orange peel and chop finely. Separate the oranges into segments, removing membranes and squeezing out remaining juice. Simmer the oranges with ¼ cup sugar, the chopped peel, juice of ½ a lemon, and ½ cup water for 15 minutes. Cool to room temperature. Place the remaining sugar in the small bowl of the mixer with the cornstarch and blend. Add the butter and beat until smooth and fluffy. Add the eggs, one at a time, reserving 1 teaspoon of yolk. Fold in the cooled marmalade mixture and the liqueur. Pour into a pie shell and cover with a lattice crust. Combine the reserved egg yolk with 1 teaspoon of water and brush the pie top with it. Bake 10 minutes at 425 degrees, reduce to 350 degrees, and bake 35 to 40 minutes or until the pie is set. Cool and serve with whipped cream.

CHIFFON PIES

A very simple but quite elegant pie can be made in infinite taste combinations, based on one of the whip-and-chill pudding mixes. For the crust use your old trusty pie dough with a liqueur substituted for the liquid. Then, using one of the no-cook pudding mixes, follow the package directions, substituting a liqueur for half of the liquid required. Too much liqueur may impair the setting qualities of the filling, but some experimentation with your brand will show how much it will accept. We most often use a vanilla pudding and make interesting taste combinations with the crust. Try chocolate filling in a mint crust. Or try peach filling in an almond crust. How about strawberry filling in an orange crust? Or come up with some combinations of your own.

We have talked about baking pie shells in chapter 1; so all you need do is bake the shell, cool it, fill it with your exotic mix, and refrigerate. Whipped cream on top is caloric but good and some sprinkles of grated chocolate or coconut still further augment the calories and eye appeal.

CAKES

With the grocer's shelves bulging with really superb cake mixes, this is no time to worry about starting from scratch. But excellent as the mixes are, some slight additions and modifications are not only acceptable but delicious. Many of the cake mixes can be converted to a Bundt recipe by using:

> 1 pkg cake mix
> 1 pkg vanilla pudding mix
> 4 eggs, beaten
> ¾ cup liquid
> ¾ cup oil
> Your favorite spice, as nutmeg, cinnamon, or allspice

We still further modify this by using wine as the liquid or by using half water and half liqueur of choice. These cakes are delightful when dusted with powdered sugar, but a contrasting frosting is very arresting. For example, we use a chocolate Bundt-chocolate liqueur cake with a raspberry liqueur frosting. Or a golden Bundt-quince wine cake with a quince liqueur frosting. The possible combinations are just as intriguing as for the chiffon pies.

The cakes are baked in a Bundt pan for 45 minutes at 350 degrees or until a straw comes out clean. Cool on a rack for a few minutes, turn out, allow to cool, and frost later, using the frosting ideas which follow shortly.

Most people wrap fruit cake in cloths soaked in brandy or wine. Sherry is good for this purpose, as is any kind of fruit wine. Especially interesting is the festive Orange-Cranberry

Wine (see chapter 16). As a matter of fact, although fruit cake mix is quite dry, the fruits can be soaked in your favorite wine and the mix can be moistened with it.

The Fruit Wine Dessert Sauce described in chapter 13 is excellent when drizzled over slices of cake, particularly pound cake. Also, made quite thick and with chopped nuts and raisins added, the sauce makes a delightful filling between layers of white cake in the Lady Baltimore style.

FRUIT TORTES

We treasure a raspberry torte which keeps for months either frozen or simply refrigerated. This makes a great dessert to have on hand for emergency use. Here, it serves as a prototype for many other varieties.

Take a loaf of frozen pound cake and, while it is still frozen, slice it horizontally with an electric knife into as many very thin slabs as you can. We usually get four layers. Make your favorite powdered sugar frosting, substituting raspberry liqueur or raspberry wine for the liquid, or use canned vanilla frosting, adding 2 tablespoons or more of raspberry liqueur or wine, then rethickening by adding powdered sugar to the desired consistency. Try chocolate frosting with either raspberry liqueur or raspberry wine also.

On each slab of the cake, drizzle a small amount of raspberry liqueur or raspberry wine and then assemble the torte as follows. Alternately, use raspberry jam and the raspberry frosting between layers and then cover the whole torte with a thick layer of the raspberry frosting. Refrigerate for a few hours before slicing to serve. Variations include quince jam and quince frosting, orange marmalade and chocolate frosting, or you name it.

FROSTINGS AND MERINGUES

We use frosting mixes because they are so good and so easy

Raspberry wine has many uses in desserts. The torte of pound cake has raspberry wine drizzled on the layers with alternating raspberry jam and raspberry wine frosting between the layers. Raspberry wine frosting is spread thickly over all. The fruit compote of the season's offerings is marinated in raspberry wine and served in a hollow-stem champagne glass. The Peach Melba has a scoop of vanilla ice cream topped with a peach half on a meringue nest with raspberry wine sauce over all. In front is raspberry hasty pudding with raspberry wine sauce.

to modify. We add any wine or liqueur, especially the latter, to the vanilla or chocolate frostings. The secret of success is to add enough liqueur to get a pronounced flavor and then work in enough powdered sugar to restore the original consistency.

The basic meringue is made with ¼ cup sugar per egg white. Let the separated egg whites come to room temperature and ordinarily they will beat to very dry stiff peaks without trouble. However, recalcitrant egg whites do better with ¼ teaspoon cream of tartar per 4 egg whites. Drizzle the sugar very slowly into the egg whites as they are being beaten. The meringues most often are baked as nests but may be baked as rectangular slabs or as pie shells. They are baked almost forever, at 200 degrees, until crunchy. Higher heat browns them in an unsightly fashion. Let the meringues cool in the oven with the door slightly open and then immediately close them in plastic bags. If they become soggy, just rebake until crunchy.

We use the meringue nests most often, filling the center with ice cream covered with raspberries marinated in raspberry liqueur or raspberry wine. Other berries, such as strawberries or blueberries, are excellent; but berries such as blackberries and boysenberries should be cooked with sugar to form a sauce as they are too sour when fresh. Add some appropriate wine or liqueur when cooking to make the sauce.

The meringue slabs are used to form elegant tortes for very special occasions. Make the slabs about the size of a loaf cake, or you can draw a circle on foil so that a "plate" of meringue results. The meringue should not be made over ¾ inch in thickness. Form the torte by softening ice cream of the desired flavor and spreading a layer on a meringue slab. Then place some fruit such as strawberries and embed these in the ice cream. Set on another slab of meringue and continue. Freeze long enough to harden the ice cream but not too long or the guests will be chasing flying pieces all over the dining room. Best get it out some minutes before serving.

The meringue pie shell is used similarly, or it may be filled with a mixture consisting of half instant pudding mix and half heavy whipped cream. Decorate with appropriate pieces of fruit and refrigerate for about 3 hours but not so long that the meringue soaks.

BROILED GRAPEFRUIT   *Sherry*

A grapefruit half becomes an elegant light dessert when the central core of pith is removed, the membranes are taken out from between the sections, and the cavity is filled with sherry. Sprinkle on some Angostura bitters and brown sugar, masking the central hole with a maraschino cherry. Place under the broiler until the brown sugar melts and bubbles.

STEWED FRUITS

We always freeze many more boysenberries than we can use in pies, but these berries are too sour to use raw as we do the other varieties. We solved the problem by cooking the berries in half water-half wine, to barely cover. This sauce is good as a breakfast dish, as a covering for dry cereal, or over ice cream at dinner. Other fruits can be treated in the same way, with added wine, and used for the same purposes. Apple sauce with apple wine is particularly good. The little extra wine flavor is very agreeable and different.

BAKED APPLE TREAT   *Sherry*

Core the apples, being careful not to cut through the bottom; then peel. Into ¾ cup sugar, mix 2 teaspoons cinnamon. Spoon 1 tablespoon of this mixture and 1 teaspoon of sherry or apple wine into the cavity of each apple. Bake an hour at 350 degrees.

Apple pie gets an added boost from apple wine in the crust instead of water and some apple wine in the pie itself. Stewed apples get additional flavor from apple wine. The baked apples have sherry in the central cavity. They are peeled before baking, in the French manner.

Baking peeled apples is the French method, which eliminates the unsightly wrinkled skin. These apples are much easier to eat also. They do not go to pieces, as might be expected. One little trick to avoid making a hole in the bottom of the apple is to core with a melon baller. Serve with apple wine sauce.

POACHED PEARS   *Pear Wine*

With an abundance of old-style hard pears, we poach and can many for winter use. Peeled, cored pear halves are placed in heavy syrup (equal parts water and sugar), strongly flavored with vanilla bean and pear wine. Cover the pears with the hot syrup and poach in a 325-degree oven for about 1½ hours. Too hot an oven will brown the pears and syrup. The halves can be put up in jars or refrigerated for long periods. They are eaten plain, drizzled with chocolate syrup, with ice cream thawed in milk, or with a scoop of ice cream. Excess syrup is used to make wine. Other fruits which will not go to pieces may be similarly prepared.

FRUIT COMPOTES

Strawberries Romanoff make an elegant dessert with great flair and little trouble. Pour orange liqueur over the largest strawberries you can find and let them marinate in the refrigerator for several hours, spooning the liqueur over them from time to time. To serve, pile the berries in hollow-stem champagne glasses and divide the marinade between them. After eating the berries, it is perfectly good form to drink the marinade. Fruit compote made from any fresh fruits or combination of fruits can be enhanced in the same way with a marinade of your favorite liqueur of contrasting or complementing flavor.

We particularly enjoy fruits and melons of the season, especially from our own garden, cut up and marinated in the almond-flavored liqueur which we make from plum-peach-nectarine-apricot-cherry seeds. This fruit macédoine is served in champagne glasses. For the wintertime, any available fruits such as bananas, oranges, and mangoes may be used. Mango liqueur makes a very tasty marinade for them.

MULBERRY HASTY PUDDING   *Mulberry-Ginger Wine*

Put about a 2-inch layer of mulberries or any other available berries into an 8-inch baking dish and sprinkle with ½ cup sugar, 2 tablespoons flour, ¼ teaspoon cinnamon, 1 tablespoon lemon juice, and a dash of nutmeg. Over this pour your favorite sweetened muffin batter. To accentuate the flavor, you may substitute mulberry-ginger wine for the liquid in the batter. Bake in a 350-degree oven for about half an hour or until golden brown and a toothpick comes out clean. Serve mulberry-ginger wine sauce (see Fruit Wine Dessert Sauce in chapter 13 and Mulberry-Ginger in chapter 16) over the pudding, either hot or cold. The hasty pudding freezes beautifully as does the sauce. We usually freeze the pudding in individual baking dishes with the sauce already on.

Although we bill this as a mulberry recipe, it is particularly good with either red or black raspberries. Use a wine sauce with whatever wine flavor goes well with the fruit in the pudding.

ZABAGLIONE   *Plum Wine*

This famous Italian hot custard dessert has two strikes against it. First, it is strictly a last-minute dish, best ordered in traditional form when dining out because at home, after a couple of martinis and wine with dinner, who wants to dash around the kitchen beating reluctant eggs over the hot stove? Second, there is always the possibility of failure, because the slightest weakening of effort or flagging strength gives you and your startled guests soggy scrambled eggs instead of a fluffy custard. Well, on with the effort!

To serve 4 persons, combine 5 egg yolks, 1 whole egg, and 2 tablespoons sugar in a double boiler over boiling water. Beat the mixture constantly, but *constantly*, with a hand electric beater until the custard is lemon yellow and fluffy. Now gradually add half a cup of plum wine and 2 tablespoons of your favorite anise-flavored liqueur. Beat madly until the custard will hold its shape in a spoon, even if this takes 10 minutes, which it often does. Serve hot in compote dishes and hope for the best. In case of failure, drown your sorrow in another martini.

WINE JELLIES

The wine jellies are made very simply by using flavored, sweetened gelatin such as jello, substituting an appropriate wine for the required water. Be sure to use your clearest, brightest wine so the jelly will be brilliant in appearance. Here again there are many combinations but the berry flavors of both the wines and jello are most popular. For color contrast, use pineapple, orange, or lime gelatin dessert. The wine may either complement or augment the flavor. Set the jelly in flat pans so you can cut 1-inch cubes. Or, set in parfait glasses, topping with whipped cream. The squares, in mixed colors, should be served in stem glasses or parfait glasses. As a great holiday present for friends, set the wine jelly in goblets or small brandy snifters.

LIQUEUR PARFAIT

Liqueur parfaits can be made well in advance and stored, covered, in the freezer for subsequent use. In the tall parfait glasses, alternate layers of ice cream with a drizzle of liqueur, using contrasing colors for the various layers. A dollop of whipped cream and a maraschino cherry complete this creation. Usually, vanilla ice cream is used but any flavors and colors are suitable.

PEACH MELBA

Peach Melba is simple but eye-catching and delicious. Cover a scoop of vanilla ice cream with a canned peach half and over this, drizzle one of the liqueur sauces, described under Traditional Orange Sauce for Duckling in chapter 13. The raspberry sauce is most nearly traditional but your favorite liqueur would be excellent. Try the almond flavor of peach heart. We suspect that Madame Melba would have approved of this.

ICES AND SHERBETS

Most homemade wines are low enough in alcohol content so that they will freeze to a fairly firm slush, making an excellent ice, if you sweeten slightly but not enough to prevent freezing. Any wine may be used. If you slowly mix sweet wine into firmly beaten egg whites, freezing this mixture, you have a sherbet. An interesting variant is the slushy frozen gazpacho which we recommended serving as a frozen salad in chapter 2 (see recipe in chapter 3).

ICE CREAMS AND SUNDAES

Softened ice cream can be streaked with any liqueur by pouring some on and pulling a knife or fork across to swirl the liqueur into the ice cream. Then refreeze solidly. Similarly, any fruit of the season can be cut up fine, marinated in an appropriate liqueur, and mixed with softened vanilla ice cream, which is then refrozen. A good example is mango cubes in mango liqueur in vanilla ice cream.

The Fruit Wine Dessert Sauce described in chapter 13 is good as a syrup to convert ice cream into a sundae. Any of the fruit flavors are good; you may like the herb or spice flavors also. We have described meringue nests with wine- or liqueur-marinated fruit atop the ice cream under Frostings and Meringues earlier in this chapter, but to mention them again is not amiss. They are worth it.

STRAWBERRY ROMANOFF FROZEN PIE
Orange Liqueur

To make the crust, you need:

½ cup butter
2 tbsp sugar
1 cup flour

Mix until a dough is formed. Roll out ½ cup of the dough and put in a separate pan to make the crumbs. Press the remainder into a 9-inch pie pan. Bake at 375 degrees, 10 to 12 minutes for the crumbs and 12 to 15 minutes for the crust. Cool. To make the filling, use:

1 cup fresh strawberries
½ cup sugar
1 egg white
2 tsp lemon juice

Put the above into a small mixing bowl and beat 5 to 8 minutes at high speed. Whip ½ cup of heavy cream and combine with the fruit mixture. Put the mixture in the cooled pie shell and drizzle 2 tablespoons orange liqueur over the filling. Carefully swirl the liqueur into the filling by drawing a silver knife over it several times. Freeze the pie 4 to 6 hours, sprinkling the crumbs over the top when partly frozen. Then the pie can be packaged and stored in the freezer almost indefinitely.

Obviously, this recipe can be modified to accommodate any fresh fruit and liqueur of your choice, but try this one first to get the hang of it.

IMPERIAL COFFEE

It probably is safe to say that any liqueur, in amounts of 2-3 teaspoons, will elevate a cup of black, sweetened coffee to gourmet heights. We use 20 or more kinds but there are some favorites such as peach heart and chocolate-cherry liqueur (see chapter 17 for instructions on making liqueurs). Some of the liqueurs can be used to give a typical regional or national flavor to coffee. For example, rose liqueur gives Turkish coffee, lemon liqueur simulates Armenian coffee, Irish mist recalls the Emerald Isles, and anise liqueur in coffee is quite Italian. Stretching a point, you might call chocolate liqueur in coffee typical of Mexico. Actually, after a fiery-hot Mexican meal, a sufficient dessert and one which quenches the fire is coffee containing chocolate-orange liqueur. Even the coffee liqueurs in coffee enhance its flavor, simulate the espresso type, are delicious, and add a velvety aromatic appeal. Tea, either hot or cold, accepts liqueurs very well. Either orange or lemon is excellent, and, of course, mint liqueur is great in iced tea.

COCKTAILS

Cocktails of great variety in color and flavor result from judicious mixing. Few people like a sweet cocktail but we have a formula which avoids an oversweet drink. The ratio is:

1 part liqueur of choice
2 parts Rose's unsweetened lime juice
3 parts gin, vodka, rum, or brandy

This gives the possibility for endless variety plus the fun of experimenting. We much prefer gin and one of our triumphs is rose liqueur, lime juice, and gin according to the formula. We have never bothered to name the varieties but leave that to you with the hope that you will not find it necessary to name more than one new cocktail in any one evening! Skoal!

Part II

MAKING YOUR OWN
COOKING AND TABLE WINES

CHAPTER 15

Basic Steps In Winemaking

We prefer to skip the erudite beginning, all about man 6000 B.C. and the bit about Cro-Magnon man quaffing wine from an aurochs horn. But we will make a few introductory comments. First, we would like to soothe those who object to wine on religious grounds. Most religions sanction it, some use it in their rituals, and it appears again and again in the biblical stories. So, there is precedent for it; even Jesus was an enologist as we seem to recall. Something about water being changed to wine. Second, we are talking mostly about wine in cooking. Even very low heat drives off all alcohol so that none of it need pass rebellious lips. So, relax; try it and you may like it—in cooking, that is.

Next, we completely disclaim even the slightest leanings toward quackery, fake cures, panaceas, and medicine show tactics. Wine does absolutely nothing for flat feet or for flat heads except possibly to make you forget them. But—and now we are talking about *drinking* wine, there are some interesting and diverse observations which may be helpful.

Wine is a good source of fairly quick energy because a 4-ounce glass of dry white dinner wine produces 110 calories. These are rather quick, easy calories because alcohol is used very directly without a lot of intermediary digestive processes being required. For this reason, diabetics can make use of wine calories. The sugar is already broken down to alcohol; so the insulin-pancreas relationship which is the seat of the diabetic problem is bypassed completely.

In addition to providing some calories, wine is a good source of organic iron for blood-building and furnishes moderate amounts of the B complex vitamins. Moreover, many wines are so low in sodium that they can be used even in a salt-free diet. Everyone knows that alcohol stimulates kidney action and, while wine is not advised in kidney disease, it is helpful in eliminating the excess water which tends to accumulate in cases of poor heart function. Also, alcohol stimulates the flow of gastric juices so that appetite is stimulated and digestion is promoted.

Alcohol in small amounts, as in wine, relaxes the smooth muscle fibers of blood vessels; so it helps relieve the blood vessel spasm and pain of angina pectoris. Thus it may have some small effect in avoiding coronary attacks. It relieves the leg pains in some arteriosclerotic conditions.

So, wine has a very good effect in geriatric and convalescent patients. Above all, it has a tranquilizing effect which reduces nervous tension and promotes sleep. Can all this be so bad?

Types of Wine

Everyone is familiar with the white and red categories of dinner wine, which usually are quite bland and mild with an alcohol percent ranging from 9 to 12. Fewer people are accustomed to the rosé wines, which differ mainly in their pink color and supposed wider range of usefulness.

Dessert wines, of which sauterne is an example, are semisweet or demi-sec, whichever way you want to look at it. These are favored because they are less apt to taste sour with a sweet dessert. They have a 9 to 12 percent alcohol level also.

Sparkling wines—of which champagne is a traditional example and cold duck is a very popular newcomer—usually are reserved for special festive occasions such as pouring over victorious ballplayers, but these wines deserve better. They are applicable in almost any situation.

After-dinner wines are the sweet full-bodied accompaniments of cheese. Port and cream sherry are examples of these fortified, usually blended wines, whose alcohol content may be up to 20 percent.

The aperitif or before-dinner wines are not popular in the United States, being supplanted by cocktails and even tall drinks. However, Campari and Dubonnet, 14 to 18 percent wines, have their before-dinner devotees.

Purists will argue that no liquid is wine unless it is made from grapes and grapes only, but these experts have the whole weight of public opinion against them. There are many other categories of alcoholic beverage for cooking and drinking, which, for want of a better name, we call wine.

It would be difficult to find any fruit, worldwide, which has not been subjected to, or even benefited from, fermentation. Vegetables have not escaped the fermentation vats, either. Everything from onions, potatoes, carrots, and parsnips to tomatoes has been used. All sorts of seeds and nuts have been employed with greater or lesser success. Flowers and all manner of herbs make good wines. Not only do grains make malt and distilled liquors, they also take their place in the list of wine materials. This does not count oddments such as honey, cactus fruit, and others. If you are interested in winemaking, you cannot possibly want for ideas as to source material.

Sweet Versus Dry Wine

A sweet wine is one with 1 percent or more of detectable sugar after completion of fermentation, while a dry wine has

less than 1 percent. This is no help, really, except as a defini-
tion, because you tell by the taste. Obviously, a sweet wine
tastes sweet and a dry wine does not. But most people confuse
dryness with acidity. A dry wine is not sweet but neither is it
sour, if it is a good wine.

Sweet wines find no place in our scheme of things except in
the cooking of desserts. Unless you want a sugar glaze, do not
use a sweet wine in cooking entrees. To sit around sipping a
glass of sweet wine is our idea of nothing to do. So, all of our
wines are made as dry as possible because we use them either in
cooking or as dinner wines.

The dryness of a wine depends on the sugar concentration
available in the must and, as this is determined by measurement,
we will discuss it in detail later.

Full-bodied Versus Thin Wine

A full-bodied wine is hard to define in really specific terms,
but the word "body" refers to the amount of the basic material in relation to the proportion of water. Tastes vary so widely
that what is a thin watery wine to us may be satisfyingly full-
bodied to you. The tendency of printed recipes is to call for too
great a proportion of water in relation to fruit so that the result
to us is a watery product. As an example of how recipes vary, we
have seen some calling for a gallon of water per 6 pounds of
apples while others call for up to 8 pounds of apples per gallon
of water. Obviously, the former is a thin wine. Again, we have
seen recipes calling for as few as 3 oranges per gallon of water
when, actually, 25 oranges per gallon or even no water at all is
more like something. We think the former is a slightly orange-
flavored, sweetened, mildly alcoholic water. Many printed recipes suggest that you can double the volume of wine by just
doubling the amount of water and sugar added. This probably is
because the unknowledgeable winemaker would rather have
twice the volume for the same cost of concentrate, and has no
idea of body. We do not want to belabor the point further

because maybe we like a more full-bodied wine than anyone else. On the rare occasions when we use a printed recipe, we usually measure the fruit with a heavy hand and withhold about 25 percent of the water. The beauty of this system is that when the wine is finished and aged, you can easily cut it with water or blend it with a lesser wine to the point where the taste pleases you. On the other hand, there is no way to remove excess water from a thin wine. Easy on the water and heavy on the fruit is a good maxim in our opinion.

Acidity in Juice and Wine

There are two general classes of acid: (1) inorganic such as hydrochloric, sulfuric, and nitric, and (2) organic such as malic, tartaric, and citric. The inorganic acids are not a problem in winemaking, but many kinds of organic acid are present in varying amounts in fruit. They are the cause of the sour taste, especially noted in unripe fruits. Usually, with ripening, the acids decrease and the sugar increases.

Producing a sour wine of high acidity is a calamity, but absence of acid is not desirable either. Acid supplies the pleasing tart taste with a tang, while a wine too low in acid has a flat, tasteless, or even medicinal character. Also, proper acidity aids in wine preservation. The bacteria which cause vinegar formation or other kinds of spoilage grow best in wine of too low an acid content.

It would seem important to measure the acid content of must as one measures the sugar content, but the measuring of acid is neither easy nor satisfactory for the home winemaker. Simple tasting is not much help either, because the acidity changes with fermentation and the complex chemical compounds present in the must mask the sour taste. Most people know of the simple test with litmus paper, which turns blue in an alkaline solution and pink in an acid one. The litmus test really is not satisfactory except for colorless must. It is obvious that a deep red must makes it hard or impossible to read a pink litmus color. Also, the same compounds which mask the acid taste may affect the color change, making it a very inaccurate indicator of acidity.

The best way to manage the acid problem is to avoid it by selecting completely ripe fruits of varieties with lesser amounts of acid, if there is any choice. For example, some apples always are very tart, some tomatoes are very bland, most pears are not really sour even when green, and so on. Selection of a proper fruit to start with is the best prevention of the acid problem.

But if the wine still is too acid (sour, not just dry!), there are a good many things one can try in remedy, some satisfactory and some to be avoided if possible. The poorest method is to add sugar and water, refermenting the wine. This just dilutes the wine, making it thin and watery, but it does dilute the acid also.

Another method is to add some chemical to react with the acid, forming a nonsour compound. For example, powdered chalk (calcium carbonate) reacts with acid to form carbonic acid, being liberated as carbon dioxide bubbles. The calcium forms compounds with the acids, which you hope are insoluble and will settle to the bottom. Unfortunately, most of these compounds stay in solution and these tend to taste like chalk. Most added chemicals subtly change the taste of the wine and not for the better. Most satisfactory of the chemicals is potassium bicarbonate because it tends to form carbon dioxide and cream of tartar, which settles out.

A suitable remedy in some cases is to blend the acid wine with one less acid, but here you need to have on hand not only a wine which is too sour but one which is not sour enough! In other words, you need to make two mistakes in order to use this method.

A procedure which works very well very often is to refrigerate the wine. Salts such as cream of tartar tend to precipitate and settle out when the temperature is lowered, forming a crust on the bottom from which the wine can be decanted. Fortunately, acidity tends to diminish as the aging process goes on; so do not be in a hurry to call a wine too sour until time has shown that it will not improve.

A too-low acidity poses no real problem because all you need do is add citric, malic, or tartaric acid, obtainable at the drugstore; or you can add an envelope of the acid blend sold at winemaking stores or by the concentrate companies.

Seeds and Stems as Sources of Tannin

It is perfectly possible to be too neat and clean in winemaking, removing all seeds, stems, and peels. This is good in preserving fruit but may not be so in the winemaking art. Wines need tannin for the slight bitter taste associated especially with red wines but, more importantly, tannin is needed as an agent which helps wine go from cloudy to clear as it matures. Also, tannin aids the keeping qualities of wine, making it more long-lived. This probably is why red wines keep longer than white ones. Unstable cloudy wines lack either tannin or alcohol or both, usually. Since fruit stems contain tannin, if all are removed, you are likely to need additional tannin.

Some recipes call for the addition of powdered tannic acid for fruits or other materials which are deficient in it. Another source is oak chips or shavings, which are added to some wines, especially reds, during fermentation. Finally, if a finished wine remains cloudy, try adding a half-cup of strong tea infusion per gallon. This source of tannin may turn the trick.

Seeds have some importance as a source of tannin but many of them such as apple, pear, plum, and peach contain amygdalin. This breaks down to release some aromatic substances, among which is the volatile oil of bitter almonds, which adds a subtle flavor treat to many wines and is not so obtrusive as to be noticed. Incidentally, do not be alarmed, but one breakdown product of amygdalin is HCN, which is prussic acid, formerly used to carry out capital punishment by gassing. Food cranks have died from eating peach seeds in large amounts as a cereal additive. In the small amounts occurring in wines and liqueurs, the flavor is good and the chemical is harmless but it is well to know what you are dealing with.

Natural Juices Versus Added Sugar

Some imported wines bear the words *"Natur Wein"* on the label, meaning that only naturally occurring sugar has been fermented with no additional sugar being used. This method is supposed to produce a higher quality wine and usually indicates the use of a more completely ripened fruit with more sugar and less acid. As we will discuss later, the sugar content is extremely important because not only does it determine the alcohol level which can be reached but it is the distinguishing mark between sweet and dry wine.

Presumably, good wine grapes contain sufficient sugar to ferment to 10 or 12 percent alcohol, but despite this statement, we note that every can of grape concentrate we have ever seen calls for rather large amounts of added sugar. As for our own grapes, of which we try to grow nine varieties in small quantities, we always have to add sugar for the simple reason that our yearly race with the raccoons never lets us leave them on the vine as long as we would like. Raccoons appear as if by magic the moment the grapes are *almost* ripe.

A good rule of thumb is that a gallon of must requires about 2 pounds of sugar, and for the sometime winemaker, it is safe to follow this guide. However, since fruit varies in sugar content from year to year, using a routine fixed quantity of sugar is not conducive to producing a predictable wine year after year. This is why we add the sugar carefully in increments, testing as we go. Adding too much sugar is easily correctable by putting in some water, which will enable you to still end up with a dry wine. If a higher alcohol content is wanted without increasing the sugar content in solution, add a pound of raisins per 5 gallons of must. The raisins give available sugar for the yeast cells, but they do not dissolve in the solution and so do not change the saccharometer reading.

Finally, some materials from which wine is made, such as herbs, contain no natural sugar and the full required amount must be added, often amounting to 3 or 4 pounds per gallon, as determined by testing. Also, such a wine has no body, only alcohol and flavor; so raisins are added for the body they impart.

Dilution with Water

The amount of water added is critical to the body of the finished wine, and it is a great satisfaction to have a general understanding of how to devise your own wine recipes. This frees you from the printed recipe, allows experimentation, and exposes errors in published recipes. There are just a few general principles in regard to adding water and these fit most occasions.

The amount of water to be added varies from none for "wet" fruits such as grapes and tomatoes, through a moderate amount for such "dry" fruits as plums and quinces, up to the total amount for the dried fruits, herbs, and seeds. It is best to err on the side of adding too little water since more can always be added later if necessary. A good empiric rule is to use 1 quart of water per 2½ quarts of fruit such as pears and plums or 2 quarts of water per pound of dried raisins, prunes, or seeds. For herbs and berries, enough water to barely cover them in the kettle for boiling, is about right.

Wine Color, Clarity, and Keeping Quality

There are some rather strange facts in regard to coloration of wine. First, the color of grape wine depends not only on the color of the grapes but on the stage in winemaking at which the skins are removed. Obviously, white grapes will always make a white wine, but a white wine can be made from red grapes if they are skinned before fermentation, because the pigment lies just beneath the skin and the interior is colorless. The great problem is that most of the flavor and sugar lie just beneath the skin also; so if you want a white wine from red grapes, you will have to add sugar. The rosé wines are made from dark red grapes, but the skins are strained out within the first few days of fermentation.

With other fruits and berries, wine color depends more on the color of the meat. For example, plum wine may vary in color from canary yellow to brown to deep red. Strangely enough, the color pigments themselves vary widely in chemical properties. For example, the berry colors remain or are enhanced by fermentation, whereas some pigments are deposited as a precipitate during fermentation. Tomato wine starts out as its own beautiful red self but as fermentation goes along, all the color falls out of solution until the final end product is a beautiful, brilliant, clear canary yellow wine with not even a hint of pink. If light-colored wine is desired, it is safest to use light-colored fruit or a dark fruit which can be peeled before fermentation. But did you ever hear of a white raspberry wine? Another answer is to put the whole fruit into the must at the start of fermentation but strain out the skins as soon as the color is just as deep as wanted.

Clarity of wine depends on several factors. There is a great temptation to put fruit into the blender before adding the yeast under the theory that if cutting the fruit into small pieces is good, cutting it into really small pieces must be still better. This is not necessarily so because the blender overdoes the idea. Blended fruit has such tiny particles that settling may be delayed for months, and filtering, which is made much more difficult, may never produce a completely clear wine.

In some cases, chemical compounds form, holding particles in suspension so that clearing is impeded. Time may come to the rescue and sometimes refrigeration may cause these chemical compounds to crystallize out. The tartar products are an example of this.

Wines which stop fermenting before completion or which have too little sugar to produce enough alcohol, remain turbid. This is the so-called stuck fermentation; this wine often can be rescued by adding a new batch of yeast. If this does not cure the evil and the problem is insufficient alcohol content, you can use the Pearson Square, illustrated later in this chapter, to determine how much alcohol need be added to bring the wine to the proper 9 to 12 percent level. Then, all you need do is add the appropriate amount of vodka or other liquor, according to the figure given by your computations.

Finally, pectin in suspension holds other compounds with it to give a cloudy wine. Sometimes the addition of Pectenzyme to break down the pectin will result in clearing of the wine (see the discussion of Pectenzyme later in this chapter under Foaming and How to Control It). As in other areas, everything depends on the proper diagnosis.

To Cook or Not to Cook

To cook or not to cook: that is the question and there is no firm answer. We sort of backed into this problem without realizing the implications. We were faced with a rather large amount of medium syrup in which pears had been cooked for canning. So, what to do? We decided to make wine of it and with the Balling measurements (see Balling Scale later in this chapter) we added enough water to give the right sugar concentration and added the yeast. The resulting wine was delightful and to our complete surprise, it had a very distinct and agreeable sherry taste. This led to the realization that sherry wine is made from cooked grapes whereas the usual grape wine is made from raw grapes. We make pear wine from raw pears, ordinarily, and the taste is entirely different. So, we decided that one advantage of cooking is to develop a sherrylike flavor. This observation has been borne out for the last several years now.

There are other reasons why one may decide to cook the fruit before fermentation. First, some hard fruits such as quinces, pineapples, and some apples, even when coarsely ground, do not give up their juices readily. The flavor yield is much better if the ground fruit is barely covered with water and boiled for about 20 minutes. Second, other fruits such as cherries, raspberries, and strawberries, not only give up more juice if boiled but the flavor is changed and enhanced. For example, who can deny that the flavor of strawberries when cooked is quite different, less acid, and more pronounced? Soft fruits such as plums and peaches can be mashed and used raw or they may be cooked for the reason which we have mentioned previously: development of a sherry flavor. The least important advantage of cooking is that in many wines, such as from the berries, the color is much more clear and brilliant after the fruit is cooked.

Obviously, the very dry wine sources must be cooked to bring out the flavor and to get any "juice" at all. This applies to herbs, seeds, and dried fruits, which should be cooked, preferably with the sugar, for about 20 minutes. This extracts more flavorful oils, softens the material for easier yeast action, causes various fruits to give up increased volumes of juice, changes or improves the flavor, and brings out the sherry taste. Whether the fruits are mashed, coarsely ground, or only quartered, cooking gives the above results plus, often, an improved color. Finally, many of the fruits and berries are less acid after cooking since the organic acids are oxidized to nonsour compounds by the heat.

Wine Concentrates Versus Fresh Material

Our interest has been largely in making wines from the products of our own yard and garden; so we adopted a sort of hohum attitude toward the canned concentrates. It seemed to us that anyone ought to be able to read and follow the printed recipe on the can, adding the right amount of sugar, water, and yeast, and letting nature do the rest. As time went on, we discovered this simplistic attitude needed some modification.

For one thing, the home gardener cannot grow the varietal grapes needed for most of the good dinner wines. Homemade wines tend to be excellent for cooking but often a little too exotic for dinner use. Who drinks quince wine with dinner? So, either you buy some concentrates or you use only the fruit-flower-vegetable-herb wines. By using concentrates, imports from many countries become immediately available: chianti from Italy, burgundy from France, and so on.

Second, concentrates may be easier to use than to prepare the material yourself. We have a huge supply of rose hips on the fence and tried to make our own concentrate. We have to admit that this was a terrible chore with many arduous steps and procedures. The end result was a dismal failure, and we went back to the simple process of buying cans of rose hip puree imported from Ireland. We found that all the mess of peeling, mashing, grinding, mixing, boiling, and what not can be escaped by the use of concentrates.

So, we ended up by buying concentrates for types and varieties which we cannot grow or obtain locally, or which we find too much trouble to make ourselves from the raw material, but using our own garden and orchard products for all the rest.

Additives

Unfortunately, most concentrates, particularly of grapes, are mass-produced by companies which are very busy huckstering all kinds of additives. We object to all the pressure, telling amateurs that they must buy and use acid blend, yeast activator, yeast nutrient, Campden tablets, sulfite solution, oak chips, Pectenzyme, fining agents, and heaven knows what else. Even when these items are furnished with the concentrate, we usually rebel and do not use them. Our lilies do not need such attempts at gilding!

We have said that we use only tannin in a few cases and Pectenzyme where clouding makes it necessary. But there are other materials which can be classed as additives. For example, one well-known author adds sliced oranges and lemons to every recipe, no matter what the source material. We think this is totally unneeded and pretentious. If we want to make lemonade, we make lemonade; but we do not need every wine to have the lemon and orange aroma.

Another common failing is to put large quantities of raisins or other dried fruit into every recipe. These dried fruits have their distinct uses, but by no means are they for routine use. Raisins make a good wine by themselves and they are good additives for otherwise thin herb wines, giving body. Also, they permit development of a higher alcohol content without increasing the sweet taste. These are valid and valuable reasons, but let us not overdo a good thing.

Yeasts and Fermentation

A detailed knowledge of chemistry is not necessary to the

winemaker, but a general idea of the fermentation process sometimes allows adjustments to be made if things start to go awry, as they often do. Yeast is a mass of millions of microscopic plant cells belonging to the fungus family. These tiny cells go into hibernation in the dry state or in the absence of food but become active within minutes if circumstances improve. Yeast cells reproduce by a process called budding wherein a piece of the cell's material (cytoplasm) gradually pinches itself off from the parent cell, grows for a short time, and then breaks off to become a parent itself.

Yeast cells live on sugar and here we must mention some elementary organic chemistry. What people speak of as sugar is a hexose, which means that its molecule is made up of 6 atoms of carbon hooked together in a linear chain with some hydrogen, oxygen, and other carbon atoms hooked on at intervals. The yeast cells form an enzyme which splits the sugar molecule into 3 equal parts. Each part has 2 carbon atoms and some hydrogen and oxygen in such an arrangement that each fragment of the sugar molecule becomes a molecule of ethyl alcohol. So, yeast splits 1 molecule of 6-carbon sugar into 3 2-carbon molecules of alcohol. During this splitting, there are some leftover atoms of carbon, hydrogen, and oxygen which form carbonic acid, breaking down to give off the bubbles which are carbon dioxide. This process of the breakdown of sugar by yeast to form alcohol and carbon dioxide is what is called fermentation. In contrast is a different type of breakdown, caused by a certain bacterium which acts on the alcohol to form acetic acid, or vinegar. The contamination of wine by this bacterium turns wine into vinegar.

From what we have said, in simple form, it is obvious that a yeast cell is a yeast cell is a yeast cell, to paraphrase one of the literati. Any microscopic yeast cell will "eat" sugar to form alcohol. It has always seemed to us that all the talk about special yeasts for special wines probably is a sales come-on or a little bit of snobbism by the experts. We have never used anything except Fleischmann's granular yeast and have no regrets. Equally obviously, if yeasts eat sugar, as they do, what is all the talk about adding special "yeast nutrients"? All they could possibly do would be to change the acid-base ratio a little and conceivably make the yeast a little hungrier so it would eat faster. We have never used yeast nutrients because we are iconoclasts who do not necessarily believe what we are told unless it makes sense.

The amount of yeast to be added has no importance except that a small amount of yeast in a large quantity of must has to go through a lot of budding generations before getting the job done. Since the more yeast, the faster the job, let joy be unconfined and add more. We use 1 envelope for a 5-gallon carboy of must.

Actually, yeast cells are everywhere around us and you cannot leave a glass of fruit juice sitting out without it fermenting spontaneously. Some feel that these "natural" yeasts are preferable to the packaged varieties; this is why it is advocated that fruit for wine not be washed before being crushed. Of course, cooking the must does away with the wild yeast and its magical properties. We have no means of knowing what types of yeasts are on the fruit or in what quantity; so we help nature out by adding the Fleischmann brand in every case. Also, we do wash the fruit, at least by rinsing off the spiderwebs and what not.

Having destroyed some of the sacred cows, to our satisfaction at least, we turn to the too, too precious arguments as to the manner in which the yeast should be added to the must, as if the yeast cared! The most pretentious method is to make a paste of the yeast, spread it on a slice of toast, float the piece of toast on the surface of the must, and pat yourself on the back for a tricky job well done. We don't bother with all this folderol. With all of the wine musts which are free of large chunks of fruit, we put the must directly into 5-gallon jugs, bypassing the open crock stage. Did you ever try to stick a smeared piece of toast through the neck of a 5-gallon jug?

Sometimes we start a yeast culture by emptying the envelope of granules into a large glass tumbler partly filled with tepid water and ¼ teaspoon of sugar. The yeast cells begin to work immediately and form a heavy foam of carbon dioxide bubbles. At this point we pour the culture into the must. This takes about half an hour and is not at all essential but it does serve two purposes. First, it proves that the yeast cells are alive and rarin' to go, although we have to admit that in using dated envelopes we never yet have seen a dead culture. The other point is that in the culture the yeast cells are working madly in a favorable medium and they tend to keep right on when added to the must whereas, otherwise, it might take them a little longer to get going. But what is the hurry?

The simplest method and by all odds just as effectual is to sprinkle the yeast granules over the surface of the must. Surface action immediately causes the granules to repel each other and spread out over the whole surface, thus giving better distribution than when a liquid culture is poured into one spot. The granules promptly sink to the bottom and disperse throughout the must. This method is our usual procedure, with apologies to the experts.

The yeast cells eventually are victims of their own appetites because, when the alcohol content reaches a certain point, the yeast either is killed or becomes inactive. This is why wine alcohol percentage levels are so constant and limited in the range of 9 to 20 percent. Sometimes the yeast cells become confused and stop working too soon, as evidenced by cessation of bubbling, a cloudy solution, and a generally disagreeable, "chemical" odor. This is called "stuck" fermentation and may be caused by too hot a temperature, too acid a mixture, or the presence of some inhibiting chemical, such as a food preservative in canned fruit juice. Usually, regardless of the cause, fermentation will start again if you simply add a new culture of yeast. Adding a fresh culture is also effective in increasing the alcohol content somewhat because, although the first culture has been killed, a new culture will work for a while and in the meantime it is forming more alcohol. This presupposes, of course, that there is available sugar for the yeast to work on. If all the sugar has been used up, adding new yeast is useless unless you add a little sugar also.

Necessary Apparatus

Although we make and keep on hand as many as 40 kinds of wine and about the same number of kinds of liqueurs, we really are very small-time operators and never make more than 10 gallons at a time. Space and our needs do not call for a bigger operation. So our list of necessary equipment is very simple.

The fruit crusher which squeezes as a lever is depressed or as a wheel is turned is not on our list of necessities. Also, since we deal

After harvesting our grapes and weighing them, we remove the stems (leaving a few for their tannin) and put the grapes in increments into a 7-gallon plastic pail, where a length of 2 x 4 lumber is used to crush them.

in small quantities and the fruit tickles our bare feet, we do not do the treading act. For grapes we use a 7-gallon plastic pail and for the masher we use a convenient length of clean 2 x 4 lumber. Soak the business end of the 2 x 4 in water so it will not absorb juice and will therefore not retain colors and tastes. For other fruits, usually coring, peeling, quartering, slicing, or pureeing suffice. Sometimes, as for quinces, we use the food grinder. Do not use the blender because, as previously mentioned, this makes the particles so small that they do not settle or filter out readily, giving a cloudy wine for a long time.

After the usual cooking in kettles, stirring with long spoons, and fermenting in 7-gallon plastic pails, the time comes to strain out the debris in a pressing bag. We use a nylon net, either fine or coarse mesh, suspended on a metal frame over a kettle or pail. For finer work, a similar bag made of 3 thicknesses of cheesecloth works well. A muslin bag gives the finest straining ever needed at this point.

We started out using glass gallon jugs but have been fully converted to plastic jugs. They are so much lighter to lift, do not break, and have no odor or taste of their own but do make it somewhat difficult to observe the clarity of the maturing wine. The plastic jugs with transparent hollow handles, however, let wine rise in these small columns, which are easy to see through. We have no need for bottles and corks unless we ever wanted to break the law and give a friend a quart of wine. The apparatus for the various wine measurements will be given later.

Primary and Secondary Fermenters

Most of the fancy apparatus for winemaking is a salesman's dream or else is applicable to those who make wine in large quantities. The important-sounding names really mean buckets, jugs, and the like. The primary fermenter is what you put the yeasted must into originally. It is a bucket or huge crock with a very wide mouth which lets you deal with big chunks of fruit and stuff as easily as possible. The primary fermenter should be of at least 7-gallon capacity because most wine recipes are for at least 5 gallons and you need room to accommodate foaming from the fruit juices. The primary fermenter can be a large ceramic crock, difficult to find anymore, or it can be a 7-gallon plastic container, made to contain diapers, garbage, or such mundane items. This container is usually covered by a sheet of plastic to keep out visiting insects, but we rely entirely on an open plastic container because we do not have bugs in our house. In the recipes not requiring pieces of fruit which make a small-necked container a nuisance, we go directly to the secondary fermenter, bypassing the bucket or crock.

For our secondary fermenter, depending on the volume of the batch, we use a 5-gallon, 2½-gallon, or 1-gallon plastic carboy. These thin-walled collapsible containers are sufficiently transparent to permit good visibility, and are light enough to be lifted about if necessary.

In our opinion, air locks are more of a fun-thing than a necessity because we know a little about chemistry. But we enjoy listening to the locks blow off while we watch a meaningless TV program. Air lock valves are some form of apparatus containing water through which the carbon dioxide gas of fermentation must pass by pressure. The level of water in the tube determines the pressure at which the gas blows off. Presumably, the atmosphere is harmful because it allows oxidation of the wine, but actually this cannot be very important. The carbon dioxide bubbles from the fermentation process break onto the surface in the jug. Carbon dioxide is heavier than air and therefore it does not tend to rise out of the jug. Therefore, it gets out only by pressure from behind as more gas forms. There is no force to pull air into the jug and actually the flow is in the opposite direction, from the jug to the atmosphere. Although we like to watch or hear the bubbling, we are completely unconvinced that anything significant is going on.

Measuring Implements

It is perfectly possible to fly completely blind in amateur winemaking, just putting the fruit, water, sugar, and yeast together, and letting them fight it out. This procedure gives an unpredictable wine, not necessarily reproducible year after year. On the other hand, it is possible to set up a small chemistry laboratory, buy a lot of equipment, and burden yourself with a library of needless information. The printed charts of measurements usually give many more data than are actually required because the range in which the winemaker works is quite narrow. While a general knowledge of the subject is helpful and comforting, it is not necessary to load up with a lot of information that never will be used.

There are a number of types of measurement which are either too complicated or too rarely needed by the amateur to warrant their discussion. For example, strict temperature control is too much trouble, color grading is not necessary, and acid measurement is too complicated. Essentially we want to know how much sugar is in solution, what the potential alcohol content is, and what the actual alcohol content is in the completed dry wine. Also, we want to follow the progress of fermentation by periodic measurement of the conversion of sugar to alcohol, to see that all is well.

To pick up the sample for filling a tall narrow testing jar, you can use a gravy baster. We use the familiar rubber-bulb syringe for testing auto battery fluid. We took out the floating scale because its figures do not apply here. To take the early samples of must for testing you need to be able to suck up some of the fairly clear solution, which is not easy because material plugs up the end of the syringe. To solve this problem push a small sieve partially into the must. This handy little trick holds the cap (solid particles on the surface) away and allows the sieve to fill with clear liquid.

Saccharometer

The essential measurement in winemaking is the sugar content at the various stages. From this, the alcohol potential and the actual final alcohol content can be ascertained. Since sugar is practically the only solid in solution in must and wine, any method which measures total solids in solution gives us a sufficiently accurate measure of sugar content. The familiar hydrometer is used but this name, which means "water meter," is inaccurate because we are measuring sugar, not water. Thus the term "saccharometer" is a little more descriptive and we will use it.

The saccharometer is a glass bulb with a long narrow tube at the top. The bulb is weighted so that the apparatus floats upright in a column of liquid. Depending on the density of the liquid, the bulb rides higher or lower, just as you float higher in salt water than in fresh water. The narrow tube contains a printed scale which shows the density of the liquid compared to the density of water, the standard. For convenience, partially fill a tall narrow glass jar with the liquid to be tested and float the bulb in it. Give the tube a twirl to clear possible air bubbles off it and to get the bulb away from the sides of the jar, where it tends to be held by surface attraction. Read the figure on the scale in the tube which is crossed by the surface of the liquid. Temperature has an effect on this reading, and most saccharometers are calibrated at 60 degrees. But if you use liquid no warmer than tepid, the error is small enough not to need correction by a thermometer.

What we are measuring by the saccharometer is the specific gravity of the liquid, which means its density as compared to water. Any solid dissolved in a liquid increases the density (heaviness) of the solution; so the denser the liquid, the less the bulb will sink or the higher the bulb will ride, to put it another way. Since water is the standard, water is given the value of 1 and since the gradations are very small, the figure is always expressed to the third decimal point. This figure is called the specific gravity (sp. gr.) of the solution. Obviously, liquids lighter than water, such as alcohol, have a density less than that of water and their specific gravity is less than 1, expressed as 0.009, etc. Must with a reading of 1.400 would contain so much sugar as to be almost solid, while 0.792 is the specific gravity of pure alcohol, which, incidentally, no one ever sees or uses. The entire scale of readings has no use for the winemaker, whose working range is limited from about 0.990 to 1.170.

While the specific gravity scale is constructed to measure density of liquids as compared to water, there is no reason why other scales cannot be drawn up to indicate other relationships directly without computation. The Balling scale is one such, made to be used in the same type of saccharometer but constructed to measure the percentage of solids (sugar) by weight. Readings on the Balling scale are expressed as degrees. For example, "25 degrees Balling" means 25 percent sugar. There are tables showing specific gravity translated into Balling degrees. By this comparison we learn that must for a dry red wine should have a starting Balling reading of 23 or 24 degrees, which is the same as sp. gr. 1.095 to 1.099. For a dry white wine, these readings should be Balling 22 or 23, the same as sp. gr. 1.090 to 1.095; while a sweet wine should read Balling 28, or sp. gr. 1.118.

There is a third type of scale which can be used in the saccharometer stem, which gives the percentage of alcohol which can be expected in the finished wine, based on starting sugar content. This is an interesting figure but fermentation, being a biological and not a mathematical process, seldom is perfect. You never get *more* than the measured potential alcohol and usually get something *less*.

Fortunately, you do not need three separate saccharometers for these three readings because the Wine-Art Company sells a saccharometer whose stem contains all three scales. So, with one filling of the hydrometer jar, you can get the specific gravity, Balling, and potential alcohol readings. Wine-Art is located at 4324 Geary Boulevard, San Francisco, California 94118, but it has franchised outlets in many cities throughout the United States. For the nearest one, consult the yellow pages of the phone book or check the phone books of nearby large cities, usually on file in your library. Also check the library for the ads in the various wine magazines.

Of course, the potential alcohol reading is valid only for the initial reading, but the others can be used in following the progress of fermentation.

The Vintech Pipettes

Instead of the saccharometer and Balling scale, you might want to use the Vintech pipettes, which are very simple to read and highly accurate in results. They are "eye-droppers" containing variously colored plastic balls, each calibrated to float or sink at a highly critical point in specific gravity. For example, when the must solution is sucked up into the Standard Vintech pipette, if 3 balls float, this indicates that the mixture will ferment to an alcoholic content of 12 percent, ideal for a dry white table wine. You can adjust the mixture to this proper reading by adding either sugar or water, as appropriate. This method can also be used to check the progress of fermentation. Two floating balls in the Standard Vintech pipette at a later stage indicate that fermentation is on its way; when only a single ball remains floating, the rapid fermentation has finished. You can rack and jug at this point. When all the balls sink, the wine is finished, indicating that all the sugar has been converted to alcohol and the wine requires

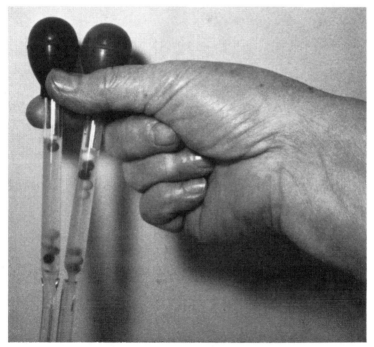

The Vintech pipettes contain colored plastic balls, very accurately calibrated to sink-float at precise points of specific gravity. One just counts the floating balls instead of trying to read a tiny numerical scale.

only aging from this point on. One great advantage of the Vintech pipettes is that, unlike the saccharometer, their readings are not influenced by the temperature of the must.

The accompanying table explains how to measure fermentation progress with the Vintech I and Vintech II pipettes. The Vintech I pipette is used before fermentation starts, in order to predict what the end result will be. The Vintech II pipette is used after fermentation has started, to gauge its progress and determine its completion. These pipettes are read by counting the number of floating balls or noting the color of the lowest floating ball. Either way is correct and gives the same data. (Incidentally, the balls in the Vintech I and Vintech II pipettes have different specific gravities from the balls in the Standard Vintech pipette; readings given by the different types of pipettes are not, therefore, interchangeable.) Charts explaining how to convert the color and/or number of balls into specific gravity and Balling readings come with the pipettes.

Vinometer

As we have said, potential alcohol content measured at the start of fermentation does not give much of a clue as to how the finished wine will end up and you may want a fairly accurate measurement. For this, the vinometer can be used, provided you are measuring a dry wine. The vinometer is very inexpensive and is made like a very small glass funnel with a long, thin tubelike tip. This tip is a capillary tube with markings on it to read the percentage of alcohol. To use it, fill the funnel with wine and turn it upside down, standing it on a flat surface so that the tube points straight up. The wine runs out of the funnel, stopping at the point where capillary attraction in the tube overcomes the pull of gravity. The higher the percentage of alcohol, the less dense the solution, the less the capillary attraction, and the lower the wine will fall in the tube. A reading at the point where the wine stops falling gives the percentage of alcohol. This is all very well and it is a great little instrument, but we do not use it because the capillary tube is very tiny and our old eyes simply cannot read the scale. It is a great thing for the younger generation, however.

MEASURING FERMENTATION PROGRESS AND THE FINISHED WINE

Color of Ball Vintech I	Sp. Gr. of Ball	Percent Sugar (Degrees Balling)	Comments
White	1.080	19.8	Minimum starting level for table wines (Balling 20-21)
Pale yellow	1.085	20.9	
Dark yellow	1.090	22.0	Preferred starting range for dry white table wine (Balling 22-23)
Pale red	1.095	23.1	Preferred starting range for dry red table wine (Balling 23-24)
Dark red	1.100	24.2	
Pale green	1.110	26.4	Starting point for maximum alcohol of 14.5% (Balling 26)
Dark green	1.120	28.5	Upper limit for starting sweet wine (Balling 28)
Vintech II			
7 balls	1.040	10.4	Strain debris from must.
6 balls	1.030	8	End of primary fermentation. Put in secondary fermenter.
4 balls	1.010	2.5	May add sugar to increase alcohol.
2 or 1	1.000-0.995	0	Fermentation complete
None	0.995	-0	Dry, finished wine

Checking the Must

Checking the must before fermentation has started lets you know if any sugar is needed and if so, it lets you measure again to see when enough is added. Or if you have been heavy-handed, you know how much water to add for the necessary dilution. You can vary your approach by measuring potential alcohol in case you want a stronger wine.

We have had good luck by using juice from the big cans of large-size Italian prune plums, put up in medium or heavy syrup. Here, the saccharometer is essential because, with the syrup, you have no idea whether to add sugar or water or how much of either unless you measure. One small problem, though, is that canned fruits and juices often have yeast inhibitors added; so you run the risk of stuck fermentation.

What to Do About the Cap

In any must which contains pieces of fruit, pureed pulp, skins, herb leaves, or other such materials, as soon as fermentation begins, the carbon dioxide bubbles cling to the pieces, causing them to float. This forms quite a dense layer, or cap, on top of the must. The cap is not harmful, actually, but has a couple of un-desired effects. First, it can be so dense that carbon dioxide is trapped under it, lifting the cap up. This may result in a messy eruption or overflow. Also, the floating pieces get pushed up out of the liquid; they dry out, the yeast cells die, and all that material becomes unavailable for further fermentation.

For these reasons, recipes call for stirring down the cap once a day or oftener in very active stages of fermentation. Stir cau-tiously until you see how much foaming up this is going to cause.

Foaming and How to Control It

Any fruit which makes good jelly does so because of its high pectin content. This is certainly no help to the winemaker because the more pectin there is, the more viscous the must and the greater the degree of foaming. There is a powder called Pectenzyme which breaks the pectin down into simpler compounds which do not promote foaming. We do not use Pectenzyme routinely, but at the first sign that the plastic pail is going to overflow, we add a teaspoon of the powder per gallon of must, carefully stirring it in. It is effective in just minutes.

There are two other reasons why addition of Pectenzyme is helpful. First, if pectin is allowed to remain, the resulting wine is apt to be cloudy for a very long time, clearing slowly or not at all. Second, in wines with too much pectin, a layer of pectin jelly is precipitated repeatedly for months and in our quince wine, even for years. This is not harmful and we even let the chunks of jelly remain for cooking purposes, but it impairs the appearance of the wine bottle and may require filtering or decanting to get rid of it.

Decanting and Filtering

Decanting simply refers to pouring wine off its dregs very carefully. Fruit and red grape wines continue to deposit sediment over a long period. We just decant into a clean jar. That always leaves a fair amount of perfectly good wine on the dregs, which cannot be decanted. We combine enough of these leavings into one jug to fill it, let it settle for some weeks, and decant again. Eventually, you reach the point where something more is needed. You can either throw the whole mess out or you can filter it.

These late dregs are in very fine particles which will not be caught in the filters used to remove the original bits and pieces left after fermentation. Most of the mesh filters are too coarse; so we use a bag of muslin which fits into and over the top of a 2-quart pitcher. Or we use a metal tripod which fits the rim of a kettle and lets the bag hang into it. For still finer sediments, a flannel bag works well but naturally much slower. In using the cloth filters be sure to moisten the bag first to get things started quicker. For the finest sediments, we use a large funnel and either the large coffee filter papers or paper towels. This is a last resort and is really slow. You use this just before saying, "Oh, to heck with it" and throwing the whole thing out.

How to Clear Wine

Before deciding how to go about clearing a cloudy wine, a diagnosis of the cause is necessary. The earliest cause of failure to clear is stuck fermentation, which prevents the formation of sufficient alcohol. Recently we made a rose hip wine following our usual procedure, but the end product was very cloudy, too sweet, and thin. Here we just added another can of rose hip puree, half the amount of water called for, no more sugar, and a new batch of yeast. This resulted in a crystal-clear, very dry, full-bodied rose wine of dinner-drinking caliber.

Occasionally a completely fermented wine is not clear and seems to lack alcohol. Here we either cautiously add sugar to stimulate further alcohol production or go to blending, which we will mention later.

The best cure for a cloudy wine which is high enough in alcohol content is the passage of time. Often it takes months for very small particles to coalesce and become heavy enough to settle out. But you have to realize that some wines, especially from certain grapes such as catawba, usually retain a hazy, slightly cloudy, tawny look.

Refrigeration, which we have mentioned in connection with reduction in acidity, also is helpful sometimes in clearing wine. At lower temperatures various chemicals fall out of solution and may clear the rest of the wine as they settle.

Pectenzyme, used to control the jelling problem, also helps to clear wines made cloudy by the pectin still in solution. The process of clearing wine is called fining. Naturally, the concentrate-sellers have tablets to add to wine for this purpose. We have some of these but never have used them.

There are several complex chemical substances which are used to clear wine. These usually depend on some viscous substance which traps floating particles and takes them down as it sinks. An old-fashioned idea, familiar to everyone, is the addition of unwashed egg shells to the coffee pot to clarify coffee. The same procedure works for wine, and since it is the small amount of remaining albumin in the shell that does the job, addition of a little egg white does the same chore without unneeded shells. Similarly, gelatin will do the same thing, as will liquid isinglass, the solution known as "water glass," formerly used to preserve eggs.

Finally, by a process called adsorption, charcoal attracts particles to its surface and holds them there. This process is used by putting pieces of charcoal into the wine and later decanting the wine. Or, you may put charcoal into the filter funnel, pouring wine over it. Ordinarily, this does not flavor the wine. If a wine is particularly resistant to attempts at clearing, the kitchen sink is always available as the ultimate solution.

Removal of Odors, Colors, and Tastes

Unless the wine is something of quaint historic charm or has some other sentimental value, batches with odd odors, colors, and tastes merit dumping down the drain because the remedies are chancy, sometime things. Best just admit failure, throw it out, and then thoroughly clean all of your equipment. Also, review your procedures to see what can be done better. Mold from dirty casks or corks, spoilage bacteria from contamination in a too-alkaline wine, improper cleansing so that chemicals are not washed away, and spoiled fruit to start with, are some of the usual causes.

Odors and tastes, often closely related, sometimes are removed or lessened by aeration of the wine. Repeatedly dip it up and pour a thin stream from a height into a fresh jug. Keep this up ad nauseum if it is getting results. A similar procedure is to use a plastic siphon tube and let the wine fall some distance through the air into a lower container.

Some colors can be removed by filtration, and all three problems may be lessened by filtering through charcoal. If it is only an off-color that is troublesome, blending with a darker wine may be a good answer. If you want to be a little sneaky and cheat a little, you could add a few drops of your favorite vegetable dye, but do not admit it.

Blending of Wines

The word "blending," when applied to wine, immediately calls up the wrong connotation; and one gets the image of adulterating quality or the reverse, adding a little good wine to some trash to make wine out of it. But by blending, we mean the mixing of two or more wines to improve the qualities in some way.

For example, a white wine of good taste which fails to clear properly or which has an off-color, can be blended with a darker wine, such as a red, to make a wine of rosé or deeper color. Then, too, with not just quite the right taste, blending may produce enough subtle change to result in something entirely acceptable.

Blending of a too-acid wine with a less-acid one will cut down on the sour taste to a drinkable level. Similarly, a too-sweet wine is improved by blending with a very dry one or vice versa. Some commercial wines, and possibly most of them, are always blended in the interests of uniformity. Sherry wines always are blended with the products from other years.

Adjusting the Alcoholic Content

Sometimes the must which you planned to ferment out to an alcoholic content of 12 percent may stop at 7 or 8 percent, which is too unstable to keep well. In this case you may repeat the fermentation process, but a more immediate result can be attained by adding alcohol in the form of vodka, for example. To do this, you may simply add vodka to taste, but this is quite inaccurate. If you can measure the alcohol level of your wine, it is simple to figure out how much alcohol to add to give any desired percentage, using the accompanying Pearson Square.

THE PEARSON SQUARE

```
A                    D
40                   5


        C
        12


7                    28
B                    E
```

A = Alcohol content of the vodka. Eighty proof is 40 percent.
B = Alcohol content of your wine.
C = Desired alcohol level of your wine.
D = C minus B, which is parts of vodka.
E = A minus C, which is parts of your wine.
So, A = 40 percent, the alcohol content of the vodka.
B = 7 percent, the alcohol content of your wine.
C = 12 percent, the desired level of alcohol.
D = 12 − 7, or 5 parts of vodka.
E = 40 − 12, or 28 parts of your wine.

Aging, Bottling, And Corking

All wines are better after aging, and many recipes set a year as the minimum time. We do not find this long a period necessary except in a few cases such as tomato or rice wine. Most of our homemade wines are entirely suitable for cooking after 2 months and, after 6 to 9 months, for serving with dinner. For example, one year we served the September apple wine with Thanksgiving dinner. All the guests thought it was a dry, fruity chablis. Aging is important in letting the full flavor develop, in reducing the acidity, and in improving the general color and clarity.

We never bottle and cork our wines but store them in gallon jugs. The wines are put into these jugs as soon as visible fermentation (bubble formation) has stopped. We screw the tops on very loosely and have no fear that oxidation will take place because the wine is not exposed to air. The space above the wine is filled with carbon dioxide, and since that gas is heavier than air, it tends to remain. The gas does not rise but only overflows. For this reason we do not worry about topping off the jugs. This is a great fetish with many winemakers and refers to the supposed necessity to fill the bottle to the top, as near the cork as possible so there will be little contact with air. We ignore this whole problem and have no trouble even with a half-filled jug. Of course, we do not make sparkling wines, in which case bottling and corking would be essential.

Also, since we do not bottle and cork, we are not faced with the possible corky taste, the loosened cork, laying the bottles down so

In the background, a colorless wine is fermenting in the plastic carboy with air-seal valve attached. The foreground bottles, containing wine which is finishing its fermentation, are loosely capped. In the plastic pail, young wine is being given some additional sugar to allow it to increase its alcohol content.

the cork will not dry out, and all the rest of the rituals. When our wines are thoroughly aged and ready for drinking, we screw the tops tightly on the jugs, if we think of it, but do not make a big deal of it.

Legal Restrictions

It really seems that many laws are deliberately made so absurd that they almost beg to be broken. Present laws on home winemaking may be on a highly intelligent basis but this is not apparent in the legal provisions or restrictions.

The government has a perfect right to require us to get a permit to make wine because alcohol is a taxable item. Actually, the form which we fill out each year is just a statement of intent, setting forth what we intend to make, in what quantities, up to an allowable limit of 200 gallons in the coming year. An officially stamped copy is returned to us; so we suppose this is a permit. However, the form contains the purest guesswork on our part. We may make 10 gallons of plum wine or we may decide not to. We may make 10 gallons of something entirely different instead. An editor writes us and asks us to devise some holiday festive wine; so we make a gallon of experimental orange-cranberry wine, for example. In other words, when the form is filled out, we have absolutely no certainty that the types and quantities specified will bear any relation to reality. We always are very far below the legal 200 gallons, if that is any consolation to the officials. Who need care if we decide to try a gallon of wine made from birdseed? But suppose an inspector-type person looked in our cellar and found more than 200 gallons. How can we prove that some of it was made 9 years ago? We could have put a back-dated label on it only yesterday. All needlessly confusing, we say!

Next, we are forbidden to sell any homemade wine, which we would not do under any circumstances, anyway, but the law further forbids giving away any wine or serving it to others outside the family. You mean we cannot serve our wine to dinner guests? Well, just try to stop us!

Then too, we cannot transport our wine. Suppose we have a friend who also makes wine. We want to exchange some of our wine with him so all concerned can realize what poor wine the other guy makes. But, according to the law, we cannot give him the wine, he cannot drink it at our house, and we cannot transport it to his house. What a business! The no-transport provision was recently modified sufficiently to permit a home winemaker to ship a few bottles of his wine to a wine-judging contest.

The most patently asinine provision of the law is that only male heads of households may make wine. A widowed lady whose late husband always made wine is cut off immediately. A liberated unwed femme is not liberated enough to get a winemaker's permit. She has to drink her father's wine. Not even her boy friends are any help unless they are married, because single men are not heads of households and so cannot make wine. But the married boy friends will be breaking the law to let her have a sip because they cannot give it away! How can anyone in his right mind keep a straight face in the presence of all this? Confusing? Yes, and a little infuriating! Do people obey this law? Well, your guess is as good as ours.

~~~~~~

CHAPTER 16

Winemaking Recipes

Most of our recipes are original but even so, they seem to fall into rather distinct patterns. So, if there is no arcane or esoteric material to reveal, we will just tell how to make each wine or even refer to some other wine where the procedure does not differ. We have not gone through other books to copy recipes, which is so easy to do, but we have tried to give our personal observations, having made and used all these wines ourselves. And so, here we go, alphabetically, because giving recipes by category or classification runs into all sorts of snags. Some slight repetition is inevitable; so try to bear it.

ANGELICA

There are essentially two ways to make herb wines. The simplest, of which May wine is an example, is to use any bland wine, add the desired herb, and then strain it out when the flavor has become strong enough for your taste. The other way is to start from scratch with basic ingredients and go through the whole fermentation process. We have used both methods and have no strong preference except that the former is quicker, easier, and a little more predictable.

Angelica is an old-fashioned biennial herb, growing in our garden; so we have plenty of material. Since the herb is used only for its flavor and has not much of anything of its own to ferment, you must add the full amount of sugar and water. It is well to add white raisins also, to furnish some body to the wine.

We use fresh angelica leaves and stems, which look much like celery and taste considerably like parsley. These are cut into inch-long segments and put into a kettle with enough water to barely cover. Boil for 30 minutes or until the stems are soft. The leaves and stems can be strained out with firm pressure to release all of the juices, but we put them through a food mill and ferment the whole mixture. For each gallon of this thin puree, add 1 pound of chopped white raisins and about 3 pounds of sugar. Be sure to check for a 23-degree reading on the Balling scale or 3 floating balls in the Vintech pipette, correcting by adding sugar or water, as required. Even though temperature of the must is no deterrent to using the pipette, it always is best to do any readings with a tepid solution. When the must is tepid, add the yeast, either granular or started in a tumbler of warm water with ¼ teaspoon of sugar. Put all into a plastic pail as the primary fermenter. Stir down the cap several times a day. Strain out the leaves and stems when fermentation slows in 5 or 6 days. Now place in water-sealed jugs while fermentation completes its cycle. Jug and cork loosely when completely inactive, clear, and dry to taste. We think this wine tastes of celery-parsley and are not able to detect the hint of anise some describe. The wine ages quickly and is usable for cooking in a couple of months although the color is still slightly tawny. This is not a drinking wine in our opinion.

APPLE

It seems simple to buy a gallon of cider at the supermarket, toss in some yeast, and end up with apple wine but it does not work out this way. Store-bought cider has various preservatives added and usually contains a chemical to inhibit fermentation since the store is not selling hard cider. Therefore, unless you can squeeze or grind your own apples, you should buy fresh apple juice direct from some honest farmer who has not added a pound of chemicals and a quart of water per apple. With pure apple juice, just add enough sugar to reach the optimum 23-degree Balling reading, put in the yeast, and you have it almost made.

To make apple wine, 8 pounds of the fruit is weighed out and peeled and quartered but not cored. The apples are ground coarsely, quickly turning brown. Some finished wine is shown to illustrate the dark color which the red skins will give if left to ferment with the must.

Apple wine has a delicate chablislike flavor, is excellent for cooking, and when aged about 3 months is a good dinner wine.

Here are two ways to make apple wine:

8 lb apples
1 gal water
1½ lb sugar
1 pkg yeast

1. Coarsely grind or chop the apples, leaving some of the seeds, cores, and stems.

2. Bring the water to a boil; add the apples and the sugar and boil for 10 minutes, removing the scum.

3. Start the yeast in a large tumbler of tepid water containing ¼ teaspoon of sugar. When it is foamy, in about 15 minutes, it is ready.

4. When the apples have cooled to tepid, take a reading and adjust by adding water or sugar to get a Balling reading of 23.

5. Add the yeast culture and transfer to the plastic pail primary fermenter. Better add a teaspoon of Pectenzyme at this time.

6. Stir down the cap several times a day and when action has markedly slowed in 4 or 5 days and the apple pieces have sunk, strain the liquid into jugs fitted with water-seal valves.

7. When the wine is clear in several weeks, decant off and let age.

In case you want to make apple wine from fresh-pressed juice, use:

1 gal apple juice
1½ lb sugar
1 pkg yeast

1. Heat the juice and dissolve the sugar in it.

2. If desired, add 2 lemons and 3 oranges, thinly sliced.

3. Adjust the Balling reading to 23 degrees.

4. Start the yeast and add to the tepid mixture.

5. Since no debris is present, go directly to the secondary fermenter, the water-seal jug.

6. Carry on as before.

APRICOT

Apricot wine is made practically the same way as peach wine; so here we will describe the basic formula, and under Peach we will give a different twist. Apricots are rather dry and fit the formula of 2½ pounds of fruit per 2 pounds of sugar and 1 gallon of water, but by all means get a Balling reading of less than 25 for a dry wine or about 30 for a sweet wine. Destone the fruit but crack some of the seeds and add them with the mashed kernel for that delightful bitter-almond flavor. Crush the fruit or just slice it, add the sugar, and pour the boiling water over all to dissolve the sugar and somewhat cook the fruit. When the mixture has cooled to tepid and you have adjusted the Balling reading, sprinkle a package of yeast over the surface. Put into a plastic pail. Your starting specific gravity should have been 1.090 to 1.095; after 6 days, it should drop to 1.040, when you can strain out the fruit and seeds. Put into a jug with water-seal valve and leave for 3 months. Then cork loosely and let age 6 months. Decant off the sediment once or twice as needed.

BANANA

Our banana wine is medium-dry, clear, canary yellow, bland, and much like a sauterne, for which we substitute it. We use both fresh ripe and dried bananas in it.

1 8-oz pkg dried bananas, diced
6 ripe bananas, peeled and mashed
1 gal water
1 lb white raisins, chopped
2 lb sugar
1 pkg yeast

Dissolve the sugar in the heated water and add all the bananas and raisins. When cooled to tepid, adjust the Balling reading to 25 and sprinkle the yeast on top. Since there is little to strain out later, you can go directly to the water-seal jug if you wish. Ferment for a week and strain. Continue fermenting to completion, bottle with loose cork, and age. Under a year old, this wine has a distinct banana flavor but after a year this taste is lost and the wine is a sauterne, fit for dinner use.

In banana wine the mashed pulp forms a dense cap which traps carbon dioxide bubbles. Stirring produces quite a gush of foam as the cap is broken several times a day.

BEAN SPROUT

This really is just a fun-wine which we made because a batch of sprouting mung beans did not seem to show much promise.

We mashed the sprouts several times and washed off the green shells. Then we barely covered the sprouts with water and boiled them for 20 minutes. To the cooled mixture we added enough sugar to give a Balling reading of 23 and sprinkled on a package of yeast. After 5 days in the primary fermenter, we strained out the sprouts, jugged the wine with an air lock, and, when the bubbling had ceased, corked loosely. This wine was clear and light yellow but had a strange taste not easily described. We let it age for a year, after which time it was bland, clear, yellow, not unpleasant, and suitable for cooking, especially for boiling with vegetables. This is not a drinking wine.

BLACKBERRY

Blackberries, loganberries, and boysenberries are completely unpredictable as to sugar and acid content. Usually, however, they are quite sour if not cooked. Since most berries give up their juices best with cooking and also have a better taste, we cook them. For most berries, barely cover with water, bring to a boil, and simmer for 20 minutes. Strain out all seeds and debris. Here, you have no idea how much sugar is in the juice; so testing is essential if you want a predictable, reproducible wine. Add about 1½ pounds of sugar per gallon of juice and begin testing to get a Balling reading of 23 for a dry wine or 30 for a sweet one. Then sprinkle the yeast on when the mixture is tepid and go directly to the secondary fermenter, the water-seal jug. Ferment till there is no more bubbling and the color is beautifully clear. Cork loosely and age for about 3 months, racking once or twice as needed. Although the blackberry wine which we make is very dry, we do not drink it with dinner because of its pronounced individual flavor, but it is excellent cooked with fowl or in the various dessert sauces.

BLUEBERRY

Blueberry wine is made in exactly the same way as blackberry wine, except that since blueberries are so lacking in distinctive flavor, they need a little help. Try adding 1 lemon and 1 orange, thinly sliced, or add 2 teaspoons ground cinnamon or 2 teaspoons of chopped fresh ginger per gallon of must. This wine is finished as are all the others and we use it with most fowls rather than as a drinking wine.

CHERRY, WILD

Wild cherries are quite bitter unless entirely ripe, when they are a deep purple-black color. We make this wine in exactly the same way as the blackberry wine above, but we crack and add a handful of seeds for their bitter-almond flavor. If this does not suffice, you can cheat a little and add a few drops of almond extract to the finished wine. This wine ages slowly but loses the bitter taste. Even if there is a little residual bitterness, it is lost in the cooking. We use it with fowl and particularly with cream cheese to make a Gourmandise-type cheese spread with cocktails.

DANDELION

The blossoms are best picked before noon, after the dew has dried. If a length of stem remains, no harm is done. Be sure not to wash the blossoms, but it is permissible to pick out some of the ants. To each quart of blossoms, add 1 quart of boiling water; let this stand for 48 hours, stirring often. Then strain the mixture, which now looks like strong tea (see the directions for tea wine), pressing out all possible juice. For each quart of juice, add 1 pound of sugar and bring this to a boil until the sugar is dissolved. Then, for each quart of sweetened juice, add a pint of boiling water plus 1 orange and 1 lemon, both sliced thin. When the mixture has cooled sufficiently, add a package of dried yeast. Let this stand for 24 hours, strain out the orange and lemon slices, and add ¼ pound of cut-up white raisins per quart of juice. Let this stand for one month, strain, and bottle with a loose cork until the wine is clear and no longer bubbles. During the following year, a fairly heavy, fine, white sediment is precipitated; so we decant the wine before use. In some of the fruit wines this sediment is pectin and other organic compounds which actually enhance the taste in cooking, but with the dandelion wine, the sediment is apt to be bitter. The important point about our dandelion wine is that it is quite dry and does not make the meat unduly sweet. This wine is not for drinking but is outstanding when used with roast fowl. It makes a wonderful crisp, brown crust with moist meat beneath.

A similar recipe with fewer steps is as follows: Pour boiling water to cover a gallon of dandelion flowers. Steep for several days and then strain. Add 3 pounds of sugar, a gallon of water, and an envelope of yeast with 2 lemons sliced thin. Ferment for a week and then strain into a water-sealed jug. After 3 more weeks, decant, cork, and await the results.

ELDERBERRY

Our elderberry bushes and our bird friends have conspired to do us out of any elderberries for the last 7 years; so we unashamedly use a canned concentrate. A quart can of concentrate, about 2 pounds of sugar, and a gallon of water with yeast will do it; but be sure to measure the sugar content to get a dry level. Some recipes add a lemon or an orange while others add a pound of chopped raisins, but this is not necessary. We find this to be a beautiful ruby-red, dry wine, entirely suitable for dinner use, cooking, or blending with mulberry to give that wine a little more character. This is a great substitute for burgundy with dinner. Only a 6-month aging period is needed.

FIG

Fig wine is quite popular, most often as a sweet, after-dinner wine. It can be made in 4 ways, sweet and dry.

1. The simplest way is to use the syrup from canned figs. The syrup is measured for sugar content and adjusted to a Balling reading of 23 degrees by adding either sugar or water as required. This wine is fermented by the usual process. It tends to be somewhat thin, but it is better than discarding the syrup.

2. We have never used fresh uncooked figs for winemaking, but it is our impression that the raw figs lack the flavor usually associated with figs. We suspect that fresh figs should be covered with water, boiled for 20 minutes, and then treated as any other cooked fruit.

3. Canned figs can be used, of course, but these should present no problems not found in fresh, cooked figs.

4. Dried figs probably are prepared from completely ripe fruit, and we imagine that the sugar content and flavor are better developed. Dried figs should be chopped rather fine, covered with water, boiled about 20 minutes to better extract the sugar and flavor, and then fermented as any other cooked fruit. The fig flavor is delicate and lends itself best to a sweet, sipping type of wine, which we do not use.

GRAPE, RED

Our red grapes have not yet escaped the raccoons and we therefore have experience only with the red grape concentrates, of which we have used cabernet, zinfandel, burgundy, chianti, and some nondescripts labelled only "red grape." Following the printed recipes is not difficult, but it *is* difficult to get a finished wine which is robust enough and dry enough to suit us. Unfortunately, the potential alcohol content rarely is attained, and it takes only a fraction of a percent of residual sugar to taste sweet. We usually cut down on the water to increase the body and cut down on sugar to increase dryness, but the red grape wine is our greatest problem. Consolation is afforded by the fact that almost none of the imported reds are full-bodied enough to suit us and few are dry enough. We look back, probably with the exaggeration of time, on the robust, dry chiantis of years ago.

Maybe we are wrong but we are not yet entirely pleased with our dry red wines.

GRAPE, ROSÉ

There are two ways to make rosé wine; we have to admit that thus far we have used the ersatz method of blending red and white wines. Our last grape crop was limited to 65 pounds for us and an untold amount more for the raccoons. We just put all the kinds together and came up with a pale red which we suppose is legitimate to call a rosé. The end result was a fine drinking wine and an excellent cooking wine; so we really have no complaint. We use the 7-gallon pail and smash the grapes with a 2 x 4 board but always have to add sugar to reach the Balling 23 reading because the raccoons force our hand into picking early.

To make rosé wine from red grapes, you have to realize that not only the sugar but the pigment lie in the layer just beneath the skin. If you remove the skin, you take away the sugar and the color; the secret of rosé is to ferment the grapes together with the skins for a couple of days or until the pink color pleases you and then strain out the skins. There are rosé concentrates which should take care of all this but we have not as yet tried them.

GRAPE, WHITE

Presumably, we grow 9 kinds of grapes, but the catawbas seem to overgrow everything else or possibly the raccoons like them least because we always end up with catawbas, which make a slightly foxy, tawny, hazy wine, good for cooking but not to suit our palates as a dinner wine. We make white wine both from grapes and concentrate. The steps and timing, whether using fresh fruit or concentrates, follow the same course. Our white wines are used for cooking, mainly with fish, for making May wine, and for making vermouth, as we will discuss later.

We use white grape concentrates in the following types: chenin blanc, chablis, and riesling. We just follow the recipes on the containers but always check the Balling reading to be sure we are going to have a dry wine. The results are perfectly satisfactory and there are no special tips.

HUCKLEBERRY

Garden huckleberries are members of the deadly nightshade family and are absolutely inedible until very ripe. In our opinion, they are not good eating even then. We were conned into planting them in the garden, where they proliferated bewilderingly. As usual, when presented with such a problem, we thought of wine.

We covered the ripe purple-black berries with water, boiled them 20 minutes and ended up with a perfectly beautiful red-purple solution. We strained out the debris, added sugar to a 23 Balling reading, put in the yeast, and let it take its course. The wine was clear, beautiful, dry, and bland but rather ordinary. We blended it with other wines of the red variety as well as some of the herb wines, producing a highly acceptable cooking wine, good with beef roasts.

LEMON BALM

A heavy crop of lemon balm threatened to completely overshadow the perennial flower bed; so we collected a kettleful of leaves and stems. We covered them with water and boiled for 20 minutes. The debris then was strained out and a pound of chopped white raisins was added. Sugar in the amount of nearly 3 pounds was added to produce a 23-degree Balling reading. When the mixture was tepid, we added a package of yeast cultured for half an hour in a tumbler of tepid water with ¼ teaspoon of sugar. Since the raisins were chopped fine and there was no other debris, we went directly to the secondary fermenter, the gallon jug with water-seal valve. Fermentation slowed in 5 days and ceased visibly in another couple of days, at which time the raisins were strained out. The wine was placed in a plastic jug and loosely corked. It aged for six months, at which time it was clear, pale, yellow-green, and dry but with a very pleasing lemon oil taste and aroma. We find it excellent on fruit compote and in iced tea as well as for light roasts such as veal.

LITCHI NUT AND OTHER CANNED JUICES

We mention litchi nut wine only as an example of what can be done with leftover syrups from canned fruits, no matter how small the quantity. We use canned Chinese litchi nuts occasionally in Chinese foods and always have the rose-flavored syrup left. All you have to do with this or any other syrup is to measure the sugar content on the Balling scale, add either sugar or water to adjust to a reading of 23 for a dry wine or 30 for a sweet wine, add yeast, and proceed as for any other wine. These wines are apt to be somewhat thin but are entirely suitable for cooking.

MANGO

We prefer the large, quite ripe Hayden mangoes, using 4 per 1 gallon of water. We do not cook the mangoes because the taste is changed for the worse in our opinion. Ripe mangoes can be peeled, cut from the seeds, and mashed quite easily. No raisins need be added. It takes about 2 pounds of sugar per gallon of fruit and water to attain a Balling reading of 23 degrees. From that point the procedure is just to add the yeast, strain in 3 to 5 days, ferment with air lock, loosely cork, and age. The orange-yellow wine ages quickly and is good in cooking meats after about 3 months.

MAY WINE

In Europe, May wine is strictly seasonal and a treat to be served with fresh strawberries in the spring. In the United

States, it is a little known specialty wine for very occasional use in a kind of punch-type drink. May wine is any mild, light, dry white wine flavored with the herb waldmeister, which we discovered is the same herb as woodruff, a wild or cultivated ground cover in the northeastern states. We planted woodruff in our forest garden several years ago and now have at least 8 times the original area densely covered with this fragrant herb. In addition, we have given several plantersful to friends and have 4 other areas of transplanted herb.

We had an extra batch of dry catawba wine from our grapes and with no special plans for it, we decided to experiment in making May wine. It seemed best to use dried woodruff leaves because they have no "green" taste. We added 2 tablespoons of the dried leaves to 1 gallon of wine and within 24 hours, the taste was strong enough so that we filtered the wine through coffee filter paper, calling it done. Undoubtedly a smaller quantity of leaves left for a longer period of time would be just as satisfactory. Probably, taste is the only way to judge when the wine is sufficiently flavorful. It is possible to pursue the more arduous route of starting from the beginning with water, sugar, raisins, lemon or orange, yeast, and woodruff leaves, going through the entire process of fermentation to end up with a "legitimate" May wine but the short-cut infusion method is quicker and entirely satisfactory.

MULBERRY-GINGER

Our untutored birds were entirely unimpressed when we planted a mulberry tree for them, and completely ignored the huge first crop. So, the next year we said, if they won't, we will! We picked several gallons of huge berries, ate some, gave some away, made pies and hasty pudding, and still had plenty to try a wine. We filled a large canning kettle with berries, added water to barely cover, boiled for 20 minutes, and strained the beautiful purple juice. The taste was too bland, like blueberry pie without lemon; so we chopped up 2 tablespoons of fresh ginger root and added it with enough sugar to give a Balling

Mulberries are cooked and strained; so the must goes directly into the secondary fermenter with air-lock valve. Must is sucked up in the syringe, and the sugar content is measured on the Balling scale in the tube of the saccharometer floating in the hydrometer jar. The scale reads 25 degrees.

reading of 23. With added yeast, fermentation went along uneventfully as we progressed to the jugging and aging stage. We were a little heavy-handed with the ginger but after aging for 6 months, the taste was good. We do not use this as a drinking wine but it is excellent in roasting meats.

ORANGE-CRANBERRY

We fell into this one entirely unintentionally. An editor asked us to come up with a festive holiday wine for the Christmas season; so, after discarding various odd thoughts as to material, we made an orange-cranberry wine which turned out to be excellent. In case you are seized with the irresistible urge to try it in an off-season when fresh cranberries are not available, there is a shortcut, using bottled cranberry juice cocktail. Be sure to read the label on the bottle, though, and do not use juice which contains a preservative which will interfere with yeast action. For the shortcut recipe, you need:

> 1 48-oz bottle cranberry juice cocktail
> 1 6-oz can frozen concentrated orange juice
> 3 orange juice cans of water
>   Peel of one fresh orange, chopped
> 2 cups sugar

Hold back on the last of the sugar until everything is mixed and dissolved. Then add sugar to get a Balling reading of 23. Heating the mixture helps dissolve the sugar and brings out the orange peel flavor a little more strongly. When tepid, add the yeast, and go directly to the secondary fermenter with air-seal valve. Continue as usual from here on.

In our family, a holiday relish of equal parts of ground raw orange and cranberries with sugar is traditional, and usually a large quantity is left over. This can very simply be turned into an excellent wine by adding water until the Balling reading is 23, then adding yeast.

If you think the old ways are best, you can take oranges and cranberries, starting from scratch. To do this, you need:

> 3 lb cranberries
> 2 doz oranges, ground
> 2 lb white raisins
> 3 lb sugar
> 1 gal water

Cook the cranberries in the water and mash them. Put in the ground oranges. Cut up the raisins and add them. Add the sugar cautiously to get a Balling reading of 23. Add yeast when the mixture has cooled to tepid. Use the plastic pail primary fermenter for 3 to 5 days, strain, jug, and put on water-seal valves. When clear and still, cork loosely and age. Excellent to cook with fowl, as a moistener for dressings, and as a base for wine sauce with desserts (see Fruit Wine Dessert Sauce in chapter 13).

PEACH

Our dry peach wine is strictly a bonus because our two small peach trees give us only a bushel and a half of fruit, just enough for a few pies or dumplings and the rest frozen or canned. We always are pleased to end up with several extra quarts of medium syrup in which the peaches have been cooked. As with other syrups, we simply adjust to a 23-degree Balling reading by adding water, put in the yeast, and away we go.

For dry peach wine from raw peaches, we use very ripe, peeled, mashed fruit, including some of the crushed seeds and kernels for their bitter-almond flavor. For each 2½ quarts of fruit, add 1 quart of water and approximately 1 pound of sugar. Start checking the Balling reading when about ¾ of the sugar is in and dissolved. Stop at 23 for a dry wine or go to 30 for a sweet one. Add a package of yeast and use the plastic pail. Strain out the seeds and debris after 3 to 5 days, jug with air locks, and finish the wine as usual. This wine is a beautiful orange-yellow color, very clear and sufficiently aged for cooking after 3 months. We do not drink this wine because of its peach flavor, which makes it unsuited for a dinner wine. It is extremely good when used with roast pork or fowl. In dessert sauces it is excellent.

PEAR

In our neighborhood, several streets are lined with the old-fashioned hard Kiefer pear trees, producing an abundance of fruit each year which is totally ignored by everyone except us. We gather pears by the bushel. Since they are so hard, they must be quartered, cored, and put through the coarse blade of the food grinder. The skins are light-colored and need not be removed. In a large kettle, the ground pears are barely covered with water and boiled for about 20 minutes to let the fruit release more juice and to give that excellent sherry flavor. When this puree has cooled to tepid, add sugar in the amount of about 1½ pounds per gallon, ending with a Balling reading of 23 or with 3 floating balls in the Vintech pipette. Add a package of yeast for each 5 gallons of must and use the primary fermenter. Stand by with the Pectenzyme; you probably will need it. Stir down the cap several times a day. When fermentation slows and the fruit sinks, the wine begins to clear; then strain out the debris. Jug with air lock valves, loosely cork, and age 3 months for a cooking wine or 6 months for sipping. If preferred, you can make this wine without cooking the fruit but you get a thinner, less flavorful product.

PINEAPPLE

For something new and different, peel and grind 5 small, very ripe pineapples per gallon of water; add half a teaspoon of salt per pineapple and enough sugar (about 4 pounds) to give a 23-degree Balling reading. Boil for 20 minutes; when tepid, add the yeast. Ferment for 3 to 5 days, stirring down the cap frequently. This must is apt to foam; so be ready with the Pectenzyme, using a teaspoon per gallon. Strain after about 5 days, jug, and water-seal; loosely cork when still. This wine ages quite slowly with a very sharp taste at first. It is usable and very good after about a year. Be sure to save the peels and core for extraction with vodka to make pineapple liqueur, a nice bonus.

PLUM

We always look forward to September, the month when the small Italian prune plums are so abundant, because then we make enough dry plum wine to satisfy cooking and drinking needs for the coming year. Usually, 5 gallons is about right, with none left over, but occasionally a bottle gets tucked away, to be forgotten for a few years. A recent discovery of a 9-year-old bottle gives evidence of this wine's good keeping and aging qualities. Any type of plum is satisfactory but the Italian prune plums are less acid than some other varieties. The final color of the wine depends on the color of the skins and how long they are left in the fermenting mixture. We have made plum wines that range from canary yellow through deep red. We quarter the fruit and put in some of the crushed seeds. Since plums are classed as a dry fruit, we use the formula of 1 quart of water per 2½ quarts of prepared fruit. One pound of sugar per quart of water is about right, adjusted to 23 Balling. Sometimes we cook the plums and sometimes we do not. The cooked product really is slightly the better method for clarity, color, and taste. We usually sprinkle the yeast on the surface of the must but sometimes start the yeast in a tumbler of tepid water with ¼ teaspoon of sugar added.

Plums form a heavy cap which must be stirred down several times a day. Also, there tends to be foaming; so Pectenzyme usually is needed too. In about a week, fermentation slows, the fruit sinks, and we strain the new wine into jugs with air lock valves. This wine is brilliantly clear in about 2 months and can be used for cooking at any time after this. For drinking, a 6- to 9-month period of aging is necessary.

All too frequently, we run out of plum wine in midseason, in which case we buy the large cans of big Italian prune plums in syrup. After mashing the fruit, we use it, the syrup, and all the seeds, and proceed exactly as for fresh fruit. Since these plums have been canned with skins on, they and the syrup are dark red; so this necessarily gives a much darker-colored wine. Also, this type of preparation gives a little bitter taste which disappears with aging but it takes longer to do so than with fresh plums. Then, too, you have to remember the possibility of stuck fermentation from the preservatives in the canned plums. All in all, this wine is just as good as that from fresh plums but it takes a little more trouble and ages much more slowly.

QUINCE

Quinces are a pungent fruit, misshapen in appearance, frequently wormy, always very hard, impossible to peel, and thoroughly unlovely when raw. But you can do great things with them! We quarter the quinces with a cleaver or heavy butcher knife on a cutting board. The quarters are cored and the bad areas are cut out. Then the fruit is put through the coarse blade of the food grinder. Placed in a large kettle, the ground fruit is barely covered with water and boiled about 20 minutes. This softens the fruit, brings out the flavor, and causes the release of more juice. Then add about 1 pound of sugar per 2½ quarts of the puree. When the mixture has cooled, add 1 teaspoon of instant-acting Pectenzyme per gallon because quinces have so much pectin that they foam more than any fruit we know of. Also, without Pectenzyme, the mixture is so viscous that it is impossible to get an accurate saccharometer reading. Immediately after adding the Pectenzyme, test for the 23-degree Balling reading, or the 3 floating balls with the Vintech pipette.

After yeast has been added to the tepid mixture, in the proportion of 1 package per 5 gallons of must, the must goes into the primary fermenting plastic pail. Quinces form a very heavy cap which must be stirred down several times a day. After about a week, when fermentation has slowed, strain out the debris and put the young wine into plastic carboys with air lock valves. When clearing and still, loosely cork. This wine does not clear completely for about a year, and its flavor does not develop much before that time either. Eventually, the wine is yellow, crystal-clear, dry, and pleasing in taste and aroma. This wine is a little too pungent to drink, but it is excellent with lamb or in sauces and frostings.

RASPBERRY

The berry wines are very simple to make and conform to a routine system quite closely. Cover the berries with water, boil for 20 minutes, and strain out the debris and seeds. Cool and add sugar to a 23-degree Balling reading, which will require about 2 pounds of sugar per gallon of juice. When tepid, add the yeast and go directly to the secondary fermenter jugs with water-seal valves. Cork loosely when still and age 3 to 5 months. This sounds quite simple, as indeed it is, with just a little experience.

RICE

We were very anxious to make a good rice wine because, having lived in Japan for 3 years, we wanted to continue to cook authentic Japanese dishes with homemade sake. Actually, this has been our most difficult project, largely because rice wine takes so long to age properly. We poured the first two batches down the drain after 18 months when they still were cloudy and sour. Finally, we have a good product, but it took 2 years of aging. The successful procedure is as follows.

Use 2 pounds of rice, either milled or brown, and 1 pound of chopped white raisins. Cover with a gallon of water and boil until the rice is well cooked and soft. Add about 2 pounds of sugar, dissolve, and adjust to a 23-degree Balling reading when the mixture is cool. When tepid, add a package of yeast. Ferment in the pail for 5 or 6 days and stir down the cap frequently. Strain out the rice and raisins at this time and put the debris out for the birds. Put the new wine in the secondary fermenter with air lock for about 3 weeks and then loosely cork.

The cap in this fermenting rice wine consists of the chopped raisins, which swell and float. Stirring in this case is simple.

Age for at least a year before even looking at it again or you may be tempted to taste it! It will be sour to taste and evil of appearance all this time. After a year, taste it with hope and charity.

ROSE HIP

There are so many ways to prepare rose hips that you have quite a choice. They may be used fresh, dried, or as a canned puree. In using them fresh, wait until they are fully red-ripe and then mash them with the end of a length of 2 x 4 as you do for grapes. If you prefer, cover the rose hips with boiling water, let them steep until cool, and then mash them. If you use dried rose hips, either your own or purchased, cover with water and boil for about 20 minutes before mashing. We find the canned rose hip puree to be the easiest as well as the most predictable as to end result. Also, with it, you are not tied to any particular season of availability.

There is no set proportion of rose hips to water but we find a quart of mashed fruits or puree is about right per gallon of water. This gives a wine of good body and color. Since rose hips have little if any sugar of their own, it takes 3 to 4 pounds of sugar per gallon in order to attain a 23-degree Balling reading. When this point is reached, add the yeast to the tepid mixture. In using mashed rose hips, where straining will be necessary, you will want to use the 7-gallon plastic pail primary fermenter; but if puree is used, you can skip this stage and go directly to the jugs and water seals. In using mashed rose hips it is well to strain out the debris in 3 or 4 days in order to avoid possible bitterness from the pods and stems.

At first, the must is a tomato-red color but as fermentation starts, it becomes a murky-milky mess resembling cream of tomato soup. Soon the solids begin to settle, bubbling slows down, and the clear rosé color becomes evident. When visible fermentation has ceased, jug, cork lightly, and age for about a year although, for cooking, 6 months is enough. This wine is so good that we use it exclusively as our rosé dinner wine and even serve it (illegally, of course) to guests.

SHERRY

As we have mentioned in the preceding chapter, our first sherry was made accidentally when we fermented heavy syrup in which pears had been poached. This first sherry was made with a 30-degree Balling reading; so it was too sweet to use as a cooking wine, but we found it comparable to the best cream sherry as a dessert wine.

The first puzzlement as to why this wine was so different from our usual pear wine led to the realization that sherry is made from cooked grapes, which is unusual. We checked this cooking procedure and found that a relatively long cooking always was followed by the typical sherry taste.

Later, we made a wine which we call sherry amoroso to distinguish it from our other sherry-type fruit wines. It rivals the best of the dry sherries in our opinion. We have long since given up buying sherry either for cooking or drinking. To make sherry amoroso, you need:

> 1 gal white grape concentrate
> 1 can Spanish fig concentrate
> 9 gal water
> 20 lb sugar
> 4 8-oz pkg dried bananas
> 2 pkg yeast

Cut the bananas in small pieces and mix all ingredients except the yeast and 5 pounds of the sugar. The mixture should have a specific gravity of 1.095 or a 23-degree Balling reading at this point. Add the envelopes of yeast. Ferment a week in the primary fermenter, stirring frequently. In order to increase the alcohol content, add the remaining 5 pounds of sugar at this time. When the specific gravity falls to 1.030, strain out the bananas, put the young wine in secondary fermenters with air locks, and set aside until the wine is clear and still. Cork loosely and age for at least 6 months. This wine will be a clear, red-brown color, and quite delicious either in cooking or as an after-dinner or dessert wine.

STRAWBERRY

As with most of the berries, the flavor which we recognize as typical is that of the cooked fruit. We have no idea how wine made from raw strawberries would taste. We usually make strawberry wine from syrup left over from sun preserving or from unneeded jam or jelly. In any event, the berries already are cooked and we just measure the sugar content on the Balling scale, adjusting with water to a 23-degree reading for a dry wine or a 28- to 30-degree reading for a sweet wine. Just add the yeast and proceed as with any of the other berry- or syrup-based wines. Strawberry wine clears beautifully and ages quickly. We do not drink it but use it mainly to marinate fruits or make wine sauces.

TARRAGON

A trip to Majorca intrigued us with numerous excellent fish dishes exotically flavored with what we finally identified as tarragon. Some experimentation convinced us that we could not distinguish between tarragon and woodruff, even though the former is alleged to have a slight hint of anise flavor, which we do not detect. Consequently, we made some tarragon wine by the infusion method which we have described under May Wine. We found it excellent in flavor and completely interchangeable with May wine. Fortunately, we grow tarragon in the garden and woodruff in the forest; so we have a great supply of both herbs. Tarragon wine is especially good with a cold lunch plate, as a marinade for fruit, and in poaching fish.

TEA

Our two white cooking wine stand-bys used to be dandelion and plum, but both had their problems. We always managed to run out of plum wine at an embarrassing time when plums were out of season. The large canned Italian prunes make a great wine but it is dark red and hardly a substitute for a white wine in cooking. Similarly, dandelion winemaking has a very short season and we were busy breaking our backs, chasing to schoolyards and such places, buckets in hand to pick dandelions, which are forbidden to grow in our yard. With dandelion wine, also, we always ran out at some inopportune moment. A flash of near-genius caused us to realize that dandelion must looks, smells, and tastes like strong, bitter, cold tea. So a small voice inside said, why not make tea wine? After all, the bitterness of tea is due to tannin, which helps in the flavor and keeping qualities of wine. As a result, we did indeed make tea wine, which we found so successful that we never have made dandelion wine again. That was over 5 years ago. Here is the way we do it.

Tea wine affords one instance where a set recipe can be followed without need to test for sugar level with the saccharometer and Balling scale. For one thing, the only immediate concentration of sugar is what the recipe calls for, because there is no variation caused by sugar from the tea itself. There isn't any! For another thing, the raisins do not liberate sugar immediately into the must; so they do not contribute to the total sugar level at the time testing would be done.

To make tea wine, you need:

> **25 tea bags**
> **1 gal water**
> **3 lb sugar**
> **6 lemons**
> **3 oranges**
> **1 lb white raisins**
> **1 pkg yeast**

1. Bring the water to a boil, drop in the tea bags and let them steep overnight. Remove and discard the bags.

2. Slice the lemons and oranges very thin, add them to the tea infusion, and boil for 30 minutes. Strain out the oranges and lemons.
3. Add the sugar and raisins, chopped fine. Let cool to tepid.
4. Add the yeast, started in a tumbler of warm water with ¼ teaspoon sugar.
5. Go directly to the plastic carboy with water-seal valve.
6. Ferment about 3 weeks and then strain out the raisins. Jug and cork loosely until all activity has ceased and the wine is clear.

This wine is slower in fermenting than many others, is slow to clear, tastes terrible for months, and needs at least a year's time to age properly. Eventually, the wine is clear, pale yellow, and mild of taste. It is now our most-used cooking wine of the white type and is especially good with roast fowl, on which it produces a wonderful crisp brown glaze.

TOMATO

You never heard of tomato wine? Well, you are not alone! We never had either until we were picking 2 or 3 gallons of tomatoes a day with stomachs and cellar full. With only two of us to eat them, we thought, wine! This resulted in a series of surprises.

Since tomatoes are such juicy berries (yes, berries!), you really do not need to add water in making the wine although some recipes stretch the material in this way. Use only the very ripest tomatoes and select one of the less acid varieties, if you have a choice. Mash the tomatoes thoroughly and put them through a sieve to remove all skins and seeds but be sure to get all possible juice and pulp. If the tomatoes seem to give up too little juice, let the mashed berries stand overnight before sieving. For each gallon of juice and pulp, add 1-2 teaspoons of salt, using less than you would for breakfast tomato juice.

Tomatoes have almost no sugar of their own; so you need to add 3-4 pounds of sugar per gallon of pulp-juice. Here again you should measure the sugar content and adjust to 23 degrees

Balling for a dry wine, which is what you want here. This is a specific gravity of about 1.095. Or with the Vintech pipette, look for 3 balls floating for a dry white wine which should ferment out at about 12 percent alcohol.

After dissolving the salt and sugar in the juice-pulp, add yeast by whatever method turns you on. Sprinkle it on the surface, start it in warm water with some sugar, anoint a piece of toast with the yeast as a paste, or try something more esoteric.

At first, the tomato must is simply sweetened tomato juice and it looks like it, but soon you get your first surprise when it becomes turbid-milky and quite vile-looking. It foams and smells bad. Then in a week or so you get the second surprise when all of the color begins to settle out, leaving a canary-yellow liquid. It still smells and tastes awful. When fermentation has ceased, the wine is a beautiful limpid yellow but still tastes terrible. Not for at least a year is this wine even somewhat agreeable but then, if you have resisted the repeated impulse to throw the whole thing out, you get the final surprise. The tomato wine is light, clear, golden, quite dry, very bland in flavor, not acid, and actually good enough to serve chilled as a dinner wine. It does not pay to jump to conclusions too soon on this wine!

VERMOUTH

Sweet vermouth for sipping and dry vermouth to use by the drop in martinis—this is the usual extent of knowledge about vermouth. Not only is little known about vermouth but there are wild stories about it. For instance, we seriously doubt that ancient monks, tucked away in some remote mountain retreat, were able to amass 100 different herbs as some enthusiastic raconteurs allege. A dozen, maybe yes, but a hundred, never!

Sweet vermouth has no place in cooking and we would not be caught dead sitting around sipping the stuff. We are extremely fussy about martinis and would not think of spoiling them with homemade vermouth, but we do need dry vermouth in many gourmet dishes. So we were faced with the challenge of how to substitute or make our own. Manufacturers do not start from scratch with vermouth-making, but rather they buy a less than first-rate white wine to which they add some secret formula of herbs, using the infusion method. And if you know the commercial world at all, you know that they use as few kinds and amounts as possible. All authors who mention the subject at all guess differently about the secret herb mix, but we made an interesting discovery. In many large cities there are little shops, usually Italian, which sell essences to counterfeit expensive perfumes and syrups to flavor Italian ices, to be used in baking, and for flavoring brandy. Among these goodies can be found a so-called vermouth syrup which embodies someone's idea of what vermouth is all about. We bought some of this and added 2 tablespoons to a gallon of white wine. Unfortunately, this made a wine too sweet to use in cooking; so we just set it aside. Within a few days this wine became very cloudy and blew its cork. This gave us the key to the problem, with interesting ramifications. When we let this refermentation go to completion, we had a clear, dry herb wine, tasting as near like vermouth as we can get without the old family secret formula. Now, we make vermouth by the gallon from excess white grape wine by this method, but we add yeast with the syrup to be sure that refermentation starts.

This process of refermentation has been very useful to us for several other purposes. Recently, we had a rose hip wine which stopped fermenting while still very sweet. On 2 subsequent occasions we added a fresh culture of yeast so that gradually the sugar was used up, ending with a clear dry wine of good drinking quality. Sometimes we get a wine which does not clear completely and seems to be weak in alcohol, although not sweet. Addition of yeast with sugar in small increments, as it is used up, gives a wine of higher alcohol content and clearer appearance.

We are not in the advertising or sponsoring business but if you are stranded in some remote spot, with no adjacent Italian syrup and extract store, you might like to write to Fioretti & Son, 1472 Lexington Avenue, New York, New York 10028. They can send a price list and will fill mail orders. We used to live near their shop and have a full line of all their syrups, which we have fun using in many ways.

~~~~~~

CHAPTER 17

Recipes for Making Liqueurs

Interesting in appearance, delightful to taste, and versatile to use, liqueurs can be made very simply from many of the herbs, flowers, and fruits from your own yard and garden. Despite their bright colors, fancy bottles, exotic names, and connotations of elegance, the liqueurs are just sweetened, flavored, alcoholic bases, most commonly vodka but occasionally brandy and even whiskey or rum. In contrast to the fermented grains, which are the beers and ales, the fermented fruit juices, which are the wines, and the hard liquors, which are distilled from fermented beverages, the liqueurs are in the midrange of alcoholic content and flavored with any one or a combination of herbs, spices, fruits, seeds, nuts, roots, berries, flowers, and all sorts of exotic oddments.

Fortunately, the basis of liqueurs which you may want to make and use is one of the hard liquors on which the federal alcohol tax has already been paid. So, there is no requirement for any license or permit to make liqueurs as long as no attempt is made to sell your product. In the most elementary terms, making a liqueur is simply a matter of flavoring a sweetened alcohol, and actually it is not much more complicated than this.

NUTS AND SEEDS

Before you show off your liqueur-making prowess to guests, you will want to make a number of kinds; so suppose we begin with the nuts and seeds, which are simple, versatile, unusual, and perhaps make the most delicious of liqueurs.

Crème de noyaux is a bitter-almond-flavored liqueur of great delicacy and many uses. Strangely, it does not contain any almonds. Peach, plum, cherry, apricot, or nectarine seeds have a kernel which contains a strong flavor of bitter almonds, and the liqueur is made from any combination of them. To crack these seeds without having them fly all over the room, put a few on a hard surface, cover with the plastic lid from a coffee can, and whack away with a hammer. Retrieve the kernels, crush or cut them into small pieces, and drop them into a wide-mouthed quart jar containing a pint of vodka, 80 proof preferred. Screw on the lid tightly and set the bottle away until you get some more seeds or until there is a strong taste and smell of almonds. When this point has been reached, filter the vodka through coffee filter paper, or even a paper towel, into a quart liquor bottle, add 1½ cups of granulated sugar, fill the bottle up with fresh vodka, close tightly, and shake until all the sugar is dissolved. Now you have a delicious liqueur which can be used immediately but which improves and mellows with age. Since sweet tooths vary, experiment with sugar content of from 1 to 2 cups per finished quart. Now you have your very own crème de noyaux, which should be colorless and clear but which may deposit a fine sediment over the months. If it offends your esthetic sense, decant carefully into a clean bottle. Usually this sediment is too fine to be caught by any filter.

A delightful variant of crème de noyaux is to use the same seeds but segregate them by kind. Do not clean the seeds; if a little fruit pulp adheres, so much the better. Crack the seeds as before but put the entire seed—pulp, shell, kernel, and all—into the vodka. Then proceed as before to strain, sweeten, and make up to a quart. Each of the fruits first mentioned will add some distinctive flavor and a light brownish pink color which is agreeable. We named these liqueurs peach heart, etc., indicating the delicate fruit flavor with the basic bitter almond. These are our most popular liqueurs.

Another noyaux-type liqueur is made by using apple or pear seeds, which have the same bitter almond flavor plus a distinctive fruit taste and a yellowish brown color. You might like to call this *liqueur de pomme*, and you will not see anything like it anywhere because this was our own idea.

If you grow black walnuts or can get some, a very unusual and delicious liqueur awaits you. Break up a cupful of black walnut meats into small pieces and cover them with vodka (about a pint). Let stand in a closed jar until the odor is strong or oil appears on the surface of the vodka. Then, as always, strain, add 1½ cups of sugar, dilute up to a quart with vodka, and bottle. This will be cloudy and oily on top at first. Filtering through paper will remove the sediment as well as the oil. Here again, the liqueur is good at once but better later. By all means do not throw away the vodka-soaked walnuts. They are delicious in chocolate syrup over ice cream.

We made a very intriguing discovery while on a visit to the island of Majorca. There, we tasted a thick, dark brown liqueur with a flavor much like bitter chocolate. This was called *palo tunel*. It is made from the long string bean-like seedpods of a tree called Saint-John's-bread or carob. It is a member of the locust-mesquite family. The tree now is widely scattered in the Mediterranean area, the Caribbean islands, and Hawaii. The seeds are surrounded by a sweetish jelly. We discovered by accident that small packets of the dried pods are sold in the nature-food stores. By our customary procedure of steeping in vodka, sweetening, and making up to a quart, we made an excellent *palo tunel* which gives a cup of coffee a thick, velvety feel and a dark chocolate flavor.

Coconut liqueur is made by whirling coconut meat in the

blender with vodka. Filter, sweeten, and dilute as usual. Be sure to save the coconut residue for use in baking or as an ice cream topping.

HERBS AND SPICES

For the herbs, use the trusty old wide-mouthed quart jar again and pack it about half full of your chosen herb. Then add the pint of vodka and let it steep, tightly covered, for a number of days. Usually a color change in the herb leaves tells you when to strain, add the sugar, dilute up to a quart with vodka, and bottle. Most of these liqueurs will be a light green color which you can enhance with a few drops of vegetable coloring if you wish. With these, there is more apt to be a sediment precipitated, and the flavor will definitely improve with age. From our own garden, we have made liqueurs from lemon balm, anise, angelica, tarragon, spicewood, mint, and woodruff. The angelica liqueur was made from stems and leaves. Our spicewood liqueur actually was made from dead twigs which were broken into short pieces. This has an almost benedictine flavor and is excellent. From the leaves, it was terrible! Waldmeister (woodruff) makes a great liqueur.

Ginger liqueur can be made from the canned-in-water ginger slices available in all Chinese and gourmet stores or from fresh ginger where available, often from stores with a Puerto Rican clientele.

Caraway seeds extracted in vodka make a kümmel-type liqueur, good for sipping or, if not too strong, in coffee. Various other spices such as cinnamon and clove make good liqueurs which profit from the addition of a few drops of vanilla.

Finally a good substitute for the South African Van der Hum is orange-tangerine liqueur in which coriander and cardamom are steeped. But be careful as these spices are very potent and can be overpowering.

One serious caution! Better not experiment with nutmeg because it contains myristic acid, a poison deadly in fairly small doses. That is why recipes which call for at least a half-teaspoon of various spices always call for only a dash of nutmeg. Extracting in alcohol may result in too high a poison level. Do not do it!

FLOWERS

The flower liqueurs are beautiful as well as delicious. Our favorite is rose, although geranium, nasturtium, and carnation are good possibilities also. Pack a quart jar half full of fresh-picked, unwashed petals, preferably picked before the heat of the day. Follow the usual procedure and you will have an unusual treat. In the case of nasturtiums and geraniums, the leaves and stems add a little more flavor than the flowers alone. Any sweet-smelling or pungent flower is worth a try, but some may be too perfumy for your taste. In the case of roses, the tea roses, fancy hybrids, and off-colors do not have much odor and do not make good liqueurs. What you want is a good old-fashioned American Beauty red rose which smells like a rose!

CHOCOLATE COMBINATIONS

Anyone who has ever eaten chocolate bonbons with fruit-flavored fillings realizes that chocolate blends deliciously with many other flavors. First, to make cacao-type liqueur, we use two methods. The simplest is to add half an ounce or more of chocolate extract to a quart of vodka, sweetening it to taste. This gives a clear red-brown liqueur of good flavor. The other method is to put 2 squares of sweet chocolate and 2 squares of bitter baker's chocolate into a blender and whirl with enough vodka for the blender to function properly. Then dilute up to a quart with vodka. Sweeten to taste. This is a thick liqueur on which some of the fatty elements float. Shaking before using is necessary. If desired, this liqueur can be filtered to give a thinner, clear product. But be sure to save the filter residue for cooking or baking or to make ice cream sundaes.

To make the chocolate combos, it is simple to mix chocolate

liqueur with any of the other liqueurs in equal parts, cherry or orange, for example. But this gives twice the volume and therefore dilutes each taste by half. We take any one of the finished orange liqueurs and add either chocolate extract or, better still, the 4 squares of chocolate to it, whirling them in the blender and adding enough liqueur to make a quart. With a little added sugar, there you are. Both cherichoc and orangechoc are prime favorites of ours often used in coffee as a substitute for dessert. Do not forget to try chocolate coconut liqueur by the same processes and you will get a real treat.

Another good chocolate combo is made by putting two tablespoons of freeze-dried coffee crystals into chocolate liqueur with a few drops of vanilla added. Then fill up to a quart with more chocolate liqueur. This is a great substitute for Kahlua, the Mexican liqueur. It is excellent to reinforce a cup of coffee.

CONCENTRATES

There are some liqueurs which are made with secret formulas. Obviously you cannot hope to duplicate them, but people have tried. Some of the winemaking supply stores carry concentrates which, when added to a quart of vodka, with sugar to taste, make very creditable substitutes. There are many of these which we do not need, but we have found strega, chartreuse (both yellow and green), and benedictine to be very good.

More reasonably priced are the Wagner flavoring extracts, which can be used either to augment your own liqueurs or to stand on their own merits. They are obtainable at many grocery stores, big department stores, and gourmet shops, and from the manufacturer, John Wagner & Sons, Ivyland, Pennsylvania 18974. If you do not grow American Beauty roses with their heavenly aroma, the Wagner extract has it. This may be a little too ersatz for you but it could get you out of a bind sometime, or would you rather do without rose liqueur? We use Wagner chocolate extract sometimes because it makes a clear solution without the trouble of filtering out a lot of debris, which is necessary if you use squares of chocolate.

The other concentrate which we use often is freeze-dried

coffee crystals. This meets the requirement of not adding liquid but supplying strong flavor while adding little bulk.

ORANGE-CITRUS

Among the most popular liqueurs are those from oranges and the other citrus fruits. These are brilliant in color as well as in taste, lending themselves to many gourmet uses.

For the simple but delicious Cointreau-type liqueur, you need a quart of 80 proof vodka, the peel of about 3 oranges, and 1½ cups of granulated sugar. Peel the oranges thinly with a vegetable peeler, not taking any of the white, bitter, deeper layer. Put this peel into a wide-mouth quart jar with about a pint of the vodka. Close tightly and let this steep for several days or until the peel seems transparent. When the vodka smells strongly of orange, you are ready to go ahead. Put 1½ cups of sugar into a quart liquor bottle and strain the orange vodka into this bottle through coffee filter paper or paper towels, to get rid of the debris and the excess oil. Then fill the bottle up to a quart with additional vodka and shake until all the sugar is dissolved. Granulated sugar is recommended rather than sugar syrup, which would dilute the vodka too much. Now your Cointreau-type liqueur is ready to use any time, but it does improve with age as a fine sediment is deposited. Just decant the liqueur off this material and you have a highly flavorful, brilliantly colored liqueur. Do not throw away the peel after filtering but chop it finely for use in baking, in frostings, over ice cream, or in any dish for which orange flavor is wanted.

A variant of Cointreau-type liqueur is made in an interesting way. Tie a string around a whole orange, leaving several long ends. Suspend the orange in a quart jar containing a pint of vodka by tightening the lid on the string ends. Do not let the orange touch the vodka. Set the jar in a warm place and leave it for a month. During this time the vodka volatilizes, condenses on the orange, extracts orange flavor, and drops back to the bottom of the jar. After you have eaten the orange, add 1½ cups of sugar to the material and fill up to a quart with vodka.

The Grand Marnier-type liqueur is made from thin slices of

orange peel exactly as in the first Cointreau-type recipe but substituting brandy for the vodka. Brandy can be used in any of the liqueurs but, having its own distinctive flavor, it sometimes covers up your added flavor or, in some cases, combines to give a disagreeable distorted taste. With orange flavor, there is no problem but for other flavors, it is better to try a small sample first to see if you like it.

Tangerines, with their different but yet orangelike flavor, make an excellent liqueur in vodka, by the same method. Mandarin oranges, a very satisfactory liqueur basis, have a flavor somewhat between oranges and tangerines.

Curaçao-type liqueur presents a slightly different problem because it is made from a special bitter orange, not readily available, but we made a great discovery which solved the problem. Most English orange marmalade is made from bitter Spanish oranges. Put half a small jar of marmalade of the bitter English type into a jar and shake it with vodka. Filter into a bottle and fill up to a quart with vodka. Since sweet marmalade has been used, less sugar is needed. Either just sweeten to taste or use only a cup of sugar. This Curaçao-type liqueur is also excellent when made with brandy.

Lemon peel, extracted in vodka, sweetened, and made up to a quart with fresh vodka makes a very subtle liqueur which is delicious over fruit compote or in coffee to give it an Armenian accent.

The rare Forbidden Fruit-type liqueur is made with your own combination of the peel of orange, lemon, tangerine, and grapefruit, with less of the latter than the others. This is even better when made with brandy. We have already discussed one of the best orange liqueurs under Chocolate Combinations earlier in this chapter.

THE BERRIES

The berries such as strawberry, blackberry, boysenberry, and the various raspberries and black currants all are too sour to use without first being cooked, but here the problem of dilution arises. If enough syrup is added so that there is strong flavor, the proof (percentage) of the alcohol is apt to be cut so low that a liqueur does not result. This is why we have added granulated sugar rather than a syrup, in the recipes thus far. However, at most grocery stores there is a shelf of fruit syrups. If these are quite thick, they can be used; obviously, thin syrups have a higher water content than thick ones and therefore usually have less flavor concentration. Or you can thicken store-bought syrups yourself by adding all the sugar they will dissolve. Then add the syrup to vodka until the taste suits you.

Another approach is to use unneeded jams or jellies. These work very well by adding a glass of jam or jelly to a pint of vodka, letting it stand several days with occasional shaking, and then filtering out the debris. Dilute up to a quart and add sugar to taste. Our best strawberry liqueur was made in this manner from a batch of strawberry preserves in which the berries got too much sun and shriveled into bulletlike pellets. This liqueur was excellent.

OTHER FRUITS AND JUICES

We have purposely left the fruit liqueurs discussed in this section until now because they require a little more discussion and a litttle more work. Thus far, except for the berries, we have used granulated sugar, vodka or brandy, and some flavoring substance. We have not used sugar syrup because its water content dilutes the alcohol and lowers the proof. However, it usually is not feasible to steep fruits directly in vodka; rather, you boil the fruit in a heavy syrup or use the syrup left over when fruit is canned. This works perfectly well and is delicious, but you must sweeten to taste rather than routinely adding 1½ cups of sugar per quart of base. For a heavy syrup, about ⅔ vodka and ⅓ syrup is suitable. Syrups which lend themselves admirably to liqueur-making include plum, pear, peach, strawberry, blackberry, cherry, raspberry, quince, fig, rose hip, pineapple, prune, maraschino cherry, and Chinese litchi nut. The cooked fruits need to be mashed, and you want as small a volume of syrup as will supply the needed flavor.

Soft fruits such as mango and banana can be mashed without cooking and can be extracted directly in vodka, thus avoiding the syrup problem. One unique liqueur, which we probably originated, is made from the fruits of the pear cactus. When mashed, extracted with vodka, and put through the sweetening and diluting procedure, these fruits produce a very unusual liqueur. It has a very distinctive raisinlike flavor and a beautiful clear nut-brown color. The red pigment of the fruit all settles out.

ODDMENTS

A few of our liqueurs are not easily classified; so we lump them together here. Drambuie, the favorite liqueur of many Americans, is within easy reach of beekeepers or of any who can buy honey, for it is made simply of honey and Scotch whiskey. Just use ⅔ whiskey and ⅓ honey, shake vigorously until well mixed, and set the evil-looking mess aside. Within a few days, a very dense but fine precipitate forms, slowly settling to the bottom over the next several weeks. This precipitate is so fine that it goes through any filter, but it is left behind when the clear golden liqueur is siphoned or decanted off very carefully. At this point the liqueur is ready to use, but it improves in clearness and flavor with several months of aging. Since there are literally hundreds of kinds of honey with varying flavors in assorted shades of color, you can make Drambuie-type liqueur entirely to your own taste. For an Irish mist type, just substitute Irish whiskey, using honey in the same proportions. Even a bourbon or a Canadian mist are good possibilities, excellent in coffee.

A typically American liqueur can be made from maple sugar or maple syrup and vodka or whiskey by the same general process. This makes an outstanding cocktail with 1 part maple liqueur, 2 parts lime juice, and 3 parts bourbon. No one will recognize any of the ingredients, but everyone will ask for more.

Instead of using a vodka or brandy base, why not switch to a different flavor with a rum-based dessert called rumtopf? For this delight, you need either a large wide-mouthed jar or a giant brandy snifter. Put in a layer of any sliced fruit or whole berries of the season, sprinkle generously with sugar, and pour on enough rum to cover the fruit. Use light or dark rum at your pleasure. Let this stand until you have more fruit, or preferably another kind of fruit, and then construct another layer, sprinkle with sugar, and cover with rum. Continue until the container is full or until your curiosity will not let you wait any longer. Spoon the fruit and some juice, which by now is a rare liqueur, over vanilla ice cream, soak pound cake slices with it, freeze the juice to a mushy consistency and serve as an ice, or figure out something for yourself. When the fruit is eaten, there is always some extra juice which is a great liqueur.

A cordial which dates back at least to colonial days in America is ratafia, originally made from native berries, especially raspberry, blackberry, or a mixture. Most often the cordial was made with West Indian rum, but occasionally with whiskey, and was flavored with cinnamon and black peppercorns.

We very often stumble onto a liqueur as a bit of serendipity from something else we are doing. For example, we slice bananas lengthwise and sauté them in butter, turning carefully with a spatula. Then we sprinkle generously with brown sugar, sautéing until the sugar melts and is bubbly. This is followed by flaming with 3 tablespoons of rum. The juice from the bananas, brown sugar, and rum is so tasty that we decided to try these flavors together aş a liqueur. We used a package of dried bananas, cut up fine and extracted in rum. We filtered out the debris, added 1½ cups of brown sugar, and filled the container up to a quart with rum. The end result was excellent to sip and superexcellent over ice cream or in coffee. Hurrah for experimentation!

Index